How to Read the Bible

The Bible Reading Fellowship
15 The Chambers, Vineyard
Abingdon OX14 3FE
brf.org.uk

The Bible Reading Fellowship (BRF) is a Registered Charity (233280)

ISBN 978 0 85746 809 3
First published 2020
10 9 8 7 6 5 4 3 2 1 0
All rights reserved

Acknowledgements
Unless otherwise noted, scripture quotations are taken from The Holy Bible,
Today's New International Version, copyright © 2004 by Biblica. Used by
permission of Hodder & Stoughton Publishers, a division of Hodder Headline Ltd.
All rights reserved. 'TNIV' is a registered trademark of International Bible Society.

Scripture quotations marked MSG are taken from *The Message*, copyright © 1993,
1994, 1995, 1996, 2000, 2001, 2002 by Eugene H. Peterson. Used by permission of
NavPress. All rights reserved. Represented by Tyndale House Publishers, Inc.

Every effort has been made to trace and contact copyright owners for material
used in this resource. We apologise for any inadvertent omissions or errors, and
would ask those concerned to contact us so that full acknowledgement can be
made in the future.

A catalogue record for this book is available from the British Library

Printed and bound by CPI Group (UK) Ltd, Croydon CR0 4YY

How to Read the Bible

the

Bible

so that it makes a difference

Michael Parsons

BRF

Contents

Introduction

This is a book about Bible-reading strategies. You'll have gleaned that already from a glance at the table of contents. It's a practical and, hopefully, helpful resource for those who want to read the Bible but who just can't get into it; for those who, when confronted with the text of scripture, are not sure what to do with it, what to look out for, how to approach it or how to get the best out of it. It has no grandiose pretensions about grappling with difficult passages and the like.[1] It is simply a book about Bible-reading strategies.

The first part, 'Foundations: reading the Bible today', unpacks an understanding of what sort of book the Bible is. It's perhaps the most theological chapter in the book. However, it is important to grapple with that question – what kind of a book is the Bible? – because the way we answer it will to an extent determine how we read the Bible and what we expect to get out of reading it. So the first chapter examines the biblical idea of revelation and concludes that the Bible is a witness to God's self-revelation.

The remainder of the book divides into three further parts. Part II is about what I've called 'macro-strategies' – those expansive, whole-Bible approaches that speak of the biblical narrative line and tell us two things: where to locate the text we're reading in that lengthy biblical story and where we ourselves sit in the narrative of the continuing divine history. Part III is about 'micro-strategies' and covers some interesting and helpful strategies for reading the text of scripture – the words on the page. Micro-strategies have a narrower focus than macro-strategies, in that the latter look at the big picture of the biblical canon, whereas the former help us to get the most out of specific passages. Part IV then suggests some things to look out for and to consider as you engage with scripture. The conclusion, 'Reading scripture, to what end?', rounds off the whole discussion and hopefully will launch you into a fully engaged reading of the Bible.

This is a resource, so be prepared to think through things and to try out the strategies as you read through the book. Though it's based on careful theology (see part I), the book is a practical aid to a more confident reading of scripture.

How to use this book

I've written this book with individuals in mind, though home groups, preachers and leadership teams will also benefit from using it. Each example of a Bible reading strategy has two components.

First, I explain the strategy and give an example of it from my own reading. I've done this as I imagine you'll do it – by sitting, praying through the exercise, reading the stipulated passage without commentaries or concordances and then having a go. I've done it this way because it gives a better, more realistic example.

Second, each strategy has a 'See for yourself' section, in which I ask you to try the strategy for yourself. Now, this isn't a test! So just give it a try. Sit comfortably, pray that the Lord will open your thinking and heart to his word and that the strategy will be helpful for that. Then read the passage two or three times slowly and thoughtfully. Apply the strategy, think out loud and conclude by prayer. (More detailed and specific instructions are given with each strategy.)

Remember that each passage of scripture has an immediate context – the chapter and the book in which it appears – as well as a much broader context in the biblical narrative. The first few strategies look at this (part II). It's always good to read the passage in its context. Though I don't mention this every time before I ask you to look at the set passage, assume that I do.

Context is vital for understanding scripture, but it isn't everything. Famously (mis)quoted texts, such as 'Be still, and know that I am God' (Psalm 46:10) and 'I know the plans I have for you... plans to prosper you and not to harm you, plans to give you hope and a future' (Jeremiah 29:11), are often taken out of their context and used as blessings or guidance today. Some people object to this. But if we look carefully at the scriptures, we'll see that these are the sorts of things the Lord is continually saying to his people and that they match what we know to be the will of God for his people in every age. So keep a good lookout for the context, but don't do it legalistically. The Lord can and does speak graciously to us in our own context today. If this wasn't the case, then each and every biblical passage would remain of historical interest only.

Also, bear in mind the different genres in scripture. The Bible is like a library with books from different authors, from different ages and with different genres. Look at the books in note 1 (page 172) for useful information on genres in scripture. The writers differ slightly, but each looks at genres, such as myth (Genesis 1, for example), poetry (Psalms), history (1 Kings, Acts), wisdom (Job, Proverbs), prophecy (Isaiah, Habakkuk), epistle (Romans, 1 Corinthians), apocalypse (parts of Daniel, Revelation), gospel (Matthew, Mark, Luke and John), parable and so on. Some books of the Bible contain different genres in them; for example, Matthew is clearly a gospel, but it also has elements of apocalyptic writing (see Matthew 24). Be aware of these differences and read each book or passage accordingly. Don't read Psalms as you would 1 Kings, nor Acts like 1 Peter. The audiences are different and the authors' intentions are not identical, but the overall biblical narrative remains the same, as does the divine author of each book and passage.

Ready to begin? Let's start with some theology about the Bible itself.

Part 1

Foundations:
reading the Bible today

As I said at the beginning of the Introduction, this is a book about reading strategies. But the question might be asked: do we need a book about them? Is it necessary to have a book on how to read the Bible? We haven't space here to answer this fully, but an introductory comment will perhaps suffice.

In his fascinating book on the Old Testament, *The Bible Jesus Read*, written in 1999, Philip Yancey makes the claim that knowledge of the Old Testament 'is fading fast among Christians and has virtually vanished in popular culture'.[2] In the same year, Larry Hart published a book in which he speaks of biblical illiteracy and 'biblical famine' in the church.[3] Naturally, both writers lament the situation.

Reflecting on this paucity of biblical knowledge, Yancey suggests two reasons in relation to the Old Testament in particular: it doesn't make sense to contemporary readers, and some passages – and there are quite a few – offend our contemporary moral sensibilities. Though he doesn't elaborate at length, he probably has in mind the wars, genocide, rape, slavery, patriarchal misogyny and the like, which appear to litter its pages.

In the years since those books were published, the church's Bible reading or biblical literacy seems not to have changed, unless, in fact, it's actually worsened. Anecdotal evidence certainly suggests that it has worsened: Christians don't seem to be reading their Bibles as they used to. Clive Field's 2014 study, 'Is the Bible becoming a closed book?', is eye-opening in this regard, as is the Bible Society's research, *Pass It On*, published in the same year.[4] Peter Phillips, the director of CODEC, a research centre housed at St John's College, Durham University, has a worthwhile chapter on this subject in his challenging book, *Engaging the Word* (2017).[5]

So Philip Yancey's two suggestions as to why Christians aren't reading the Bible still seem to be valid decades later. And, of course, these are two crucial areas of difficulty. However, on another level entirely, there is also a kind of shyness about getting to grips with the text of scripture, perhaps an unacknowledged sense of not quite knowing what to do to engage with the text itself. And we must be aware that engaging with the text is not the same as simply reading the text.

As we move towards unpacking that pivotal idea, let's look at what kind of book the Bible is. What is its intrinsic nature?

1

What kind of book is the Bible?

In the past, when this question was asked, we would nearly always begin by explaining that the Bible is a kind of library of books written over centuries by various and diverse human writers and inspired by God, its divine author. This latter assertion, specifically, would give the Bible its authority – these are words from none other than the sovereign God. But this would also imply that the Bible is both inerrant (biblical accuracy) and infallible (biblical trustworthiness), because God, naturally taking precedence over the human authors, was involved in its creation; being the God of truth, it would be argued, he simply would not lie nor allow human error to sully its pages. The Bible was said to be true, therefore, in the sense that it was 100% 'accurate' or 'inerrant'.

For some, this has become an entrenched position, especially because several seminal theologians of the church – including Augustine, Aquinas, Luther and Calvin – have in the past argued this, sometimes using the Latin term *dictate* to suggest a mechanism for the God–human working relationship in creating the Bible. Today, many would suggest that there is no need to travel this route; indeed, it may be ill-considered to do so. It simply doesn't seem appropriate or necessary in the light of what the Bible is.

We notice, first, that the Bible is a created thing. Coming after the fall, it takes on the fragility, limitations and fallenness of the world in which we live and of the authors, editors and preservers who brought it into being, maintained it and curated it. The great 20th-century Swiss theologian Karl Barth touches on the human quality and limitation of the biblical authors in his usual taut manner in his discussion of the first chapter of John's gospel. He speaks of the historicity and specificity of the gospel writer's situation: 'He is still a man,' he concludes. And because of this, 'He has not said it as it *is* but as he could.'[6] The truth of the Bible's message – the self-revelation of God, his salvation in Jesus Christ, the work of the Holy Spirit in the church and the world – is too grand and inexplicable for human authors to fully conceive of, so they write as they can, but they cannot convey it in its entirety or in the hiddenness of its mystery. In Barth's phrase, the biblical writer 'does not proclaim God without God'[7] – indeed, I would emphasise, he cannot.

God, then, is somehow involved in the Bible's authorship. That's partly why we sometimes use the phrase 'the word of God' to describe the Bible. Many theologians today take Barth's theological conclusion into account, in which he suggests a threefold use for the term 'the word of God'. Its primary form is as the incarnate Christ, the Son of God, who in his actions and words is the very self-expression of the living God. For this reason, all the scriptures find their interest in Jesus Christ himself; he is their centre or focal point. The secondary form of the word of God is the scriptures themselves. As we'll see, they bear witness to God's self-revelation. The third form of the word, according to Barth, is preaching which witnesses to, proclaims and applies the word to contemporary contexts.[8] On the other hand, Gordon Spykman suggests a different set of three forms: the creational word, both in the creation of things and their sustaining; the incarnate word (John 1:14; Revelation 19:11–13); and the inscripturated word, the Bible.[9] Whichever suggestion you take, you'll notice that the Bible is not the primary form of God's word – it is the second or third one. And indeed the Bible often speaks of God's actual spoken words as 'the word of the Lord' (see, for example, Jeremiah 1:2).

In spite of its clearly human qualities, its diverse historical, linguistic and cultural settings, Christians have always rightly argued that scripture in some way reflects divine speech. Eugene Peterson, the author of *The Message* translation of the Bible, says, 'God is somehow or other responsible for this book in a revelatory way.' It has the 'authorial presence of God', he affirms.[10] It's uncertain what this actually means or implies, however – hence the imprecise wording, 'somehow or other' – but it does convey something of the Bible's own witness; see, for example, 2 Timothy 3:16, 'All Scripture is God-breathed', and 2 Peter 1:21, 'Prophets, though human, spoke from God as they were carried along by the Holy Spirit.' We'll look at these verses again below, but for now we note that they speak strongly of God's intimate and creative involvement in the writing of scripture, or at least, in this context, the Old Testament.

The Bible as witness to revelation

So what kind of a book is the Bible? When we think of the Bible, various and diverse models or images are usefully employed to convey what kind of book it is. For example, Geoffrey Wainwright uses the image of sacrament. The Bible, he says, is an external sign of an inward grace, just as the Lord's Supper and baptism are. The Lord's Supper, or the Eucharist, is an external sign of the presence of Jesus Christ in the body of the church and at the feast. We come to that sacrament confident that there, by faith, we meet with the risen Lord Jesus. He is present by his Spirit as we worship, faithfully taking bread and wine. In baptism, too, no matter what mode or theological persuasion we hold, we say that we meet the risen Lord as we confess faith in him. Nearly every Christian tradition holds to this. So, according to Wainwright, in this sense, the Bible is also a sacrament: 'Both in its resting position and even more in its liturgical use,' he says, 'the Bible as an actual book serves as some kind of sacrament of the Word of God.'[11] Notice the words 'the Bible as an actual book'. He is speaking of the printed page; the physical (or digitalised) words as they are bound and read. 'The Bible,' he says later, 'mediates the

Word of God' in a similar way to the other sacraments of the church.[12] In and through the Bible we meet with the risen Christ, the living Word of God. This, he says, is a faith position: 'We must trust God at the least to have overseen the provision of an adequate foundational source.'[13]

Peter Phillips, on the other hand, in a more mundane metaphor, likens the Bible to an engine that drives us into our discipleship. Having acknowledged other models, including the Bible as a sacred artefact and as an object of study, Phillips outlines his understanding of the scriptures as a means of grace;[14] it is active, helping us to encounter the God behind its words; it 'seems to act as an engine pushing us in that direction'.[15] His thought-provoking book is energised by this theme or model, with chapters on discipleship itself, on spirituality, on church community and on our mission to the world. The imagery of an engine certainly works well. The Bible, he says, drives us to 'reach up', to 'reach in' and to 'reach out' as the Holy Spirit applies its words to our own lives, to congregations and to the contemporary world. It is a crucial part of the active process by which we receive divine grace and transformation into the image of Jesus.

These models – the Bible as a sacrament, a meeting place between God and his people through Jesus Christ, and the Bible as an engine, driving us into discipleship and holiness – are relevant and worthwhile, and they warrant further thought. But I'd like to suggest another model, which seems to me to get closer to the heart of what kind of book the Bible is. It's this: the Bible is a witness to revelation. More specifically, the Bible is a witness to God's self-revelation. But what do we mean by revelation in this context? And what is intended by the biblical concept of witness? Let's start with the biblical idea of revelation.

Revelation

In everyday conversation we would use the word 'revelation' to indicate an uncovering or an unveiling of something previously unknown. News headlines might begin, 'New revelations about...'. This is the foundational idea of revelation in scripture. The prophet's words exemplify this:

> For what they were not told, they will see,
>   and what they have not heard, they will understand.
> ISAIAH 52:15

In our understanding of God and his relationship to the world, we see that divine revelation – uncovering or unveiling – indicates a saving or reconciling movement of God towards humanity and all created things. That is, God's self-communication is an essential part of his gracious establishment of the fellowship that he wants to have with humanity in the context of the whole of creation. In that context, it should be noted that all revelation is salvific – it has to do with the salvation of God's world by God. With this in mind, the evangelical theologian Millard Erickson defines revelation as 'God's communication to man [sic] of truth that he needs to know *in order to relate properly to God*' – though he seems to over-emphasise 'truth' or propositions over against the person of God himself.[16]

Essentially, God reveals *himself* to us. It's important to notice that revelation *always* begins with the divine intention towards us and never the other way around. This is an assertion worth underlining, for it will help us to read the Bible in the way it is intended. Because of who God is, revelation originates always with him and never with us. Wolfhart Pannenberg, the great 20th-century systematic theologian, emphasises this: 'God can be known only if he gives himself to be known'; 'In revealing himself, God reveals *himself*... the revelation has to be outward.'[17] So revelation, the disclosure of who God is and his intention in Jesus Christ, is clearly an act of divine grace moving outward, from God to us.[18]

We can show this in diagrammatic form as follows:

> **Revealer** (God; specifically, the Logos: see John 1:1–5)
>
> **Revelation** (What is revealed? Both the relationship and the content)
>
> **Revelation** (The process of revelation)
>
> **Recipients** (Israel, the church, individuals, the world)

The Lord reveals himself and his ways. We are encouraged by the prophet Jeremiah, for example, to exalt in this very thing:

> 'Let those who boast boast about this:
>   that they understand and know me,
> that I am the Lord, who exercises kindness,
>   justice and righteousness on earth,
>   for in these I delight,'
>   declares the Lord.
>
> JEREMIAH 9:24

How does God reveal himself? He does so in word, in historical act, in visions, in dreams, in other various and diverse ways, and supremely in his Son, Jesus Christ. But in every single instance revelation originates and comes from the gracious God to us; it is never the other way around. We simply cannot think ourselves to an understanding of God or to a relationship with him or to insight into his ways.

Isaiah 6 is a good example of the Lord revealing himself to a single person, in this case the Hebrew prophet Isaiah. God gives him a vision into which the prophet moves ('I saw the Lord seated on a throne, high and exalted', 6:1), and God speaks to him, first through one of the mysterious worshipping seraphs ('Your guilt is taken away and your sin atoned for', 6:7) and then directly ('Then I heard the voice of the Lord saying, "Whom shall I send? And who will go for us?"', 6:8). The prophet responds in courageous and faithful fashion ('Here am I. Send me!', 6:8). Before recommissioning Isaiah to his prophetic task, then, the Lord reveals himself – both in contrast to Israel's diminished and perhaps domesticated picture of God, and in moral and evidently precarious contrast to Isaiah and the people of Israel in their sin and guilt: 'I am ruined!' Isaiah says. 'For I am a man of unclean lips, and I live among a people of unclean lips, and my eyes have seen the King, the Lord Almighty' (6:5). You might like to think about similar disclosures to the prophet Jeremiah (Jeremiah 1:1–10) and to the New Testament seer John on the island of Patmos (Revelation 1).

A key and crucial Old Testament paradigmatic revelatory event is the exodus, in which the Lord reveals who he is both through powerful and miraculous action and through speech. The miraculous plagues, the passover, the people leaving Egypt and the crossing of the Red Sea all speak of God's being and of his salvific intention towards the Israelites. Complementary to the disclosure through historical acts, the Lord speaks words of revelation to Israel: 'Stand firm and you will see the deliverance the Lord will bring you today,' he assures them (Exodus 14:13). Even the Egyptians will know something of Israel's God, the true God: they will know that he is the Lord (Exodus 14:4). Immediately after the defeat of Pharaoh, Moses and the Israelites celebrate the Lord's salvation in song: 'The Lord is my strength and my defence; he has become my salvation… The Lord is a warrior; the Lord is his name' (Exodus 15:2–3). They have learned an important truth – truth graciously revealed to them that will repeat itself time and time again in national and personal consciousness:

> In your unfailing love you will lead
> the people you have redeemed.
> In your strength you will guide them
> to your holy dwelling.
> EXODUS 15:13

Notice how specific, historical revelation becomes over time the basis for a universal truth. God demonstrates his unchangeable nature through local events. The exodus paradigm, revealing something of God and his gracious redemption, repeats itself in biblical history and instruction. For example, elsewhere, Moses, speaking of the event, says to the Israelites: 'You were shown these things so that you might know that the Lord is God; besides him there is no other' (Deuteronomy 4:35; see v. 39). Through the experience of exodus, they learned who God is for them: that he loves them as an elect or chosen people, that he set them apart from other nations and that the covenant Lord is faithful (Deuteronomy 7:6–9). In later Hebrew consciousness, both individual and communal, the exodus paradigm reappears in forceful image (e.g. Psalms 42:7; 93:3–4).

So revelation comes from God; it is in that sense always gracious self-revelation. It comes to us by divine word and action; it is salvation disclosure. Undoubtedly, the crux and pinnacle of divine revelation is in the Son, Jesus Christ. The writer to the Hebrews begins his letter with the declaration that in the past God spoke through intermediaries, the prophets, but today (a day he declares elsewhere to be of salvific significance, Hebrews 3:15) 'he has spoken to us by his Son' (Hebrews 1:2). It's an amazing thing that God speaks to his creation, given who he is, but he does; and he does that in these final days through Jesus Christ – through his life, his death and resurrection, his words and his gracious Spirit-filled ministry. Similarly, the apostle Paul speaks of this in his doxology at the end of his letter to the Roman church:

> Now to him who is able to establish you in accordance with my gospel, the message I proclaim about Jesus Christ, in keeping with *the revelation of the mystery hidden for long ages past*, but *now revealed* and made known through the prophetic writings by the command of the eternal God, so that all the Gentiles might come to faith and obedience – to the only wise God be glory forever through Jesus Christ! Amen.
> ROMANS 16:25–27 (italics added)

Again, we see that revelation comes from God ('by the command of the eternal God'), that it refers to relationship with him ('that all the Gentiles might come to faith and obedience') and that Jesus Christ is absolutely central to it ('the message I proclaim about Jesus Christ').

The definitive passage is found at the opening of John's wonderful telling of Jesus' life. In Jesus Christ was light and life, grace and truth, he tells us. The Word was made flesh, dwelling among humanity and, crucially, making the invisible God known (John 1:4–5, 14, 17). Indeed, as Paul puts it most forcefully to the Colossian church, 'The Son is the image of the invisible God' (Colossians 1:15). The writer to the Hebrews speaks of Christ as 'the exact representation of [God's] being' (Hebrews 1:3). To look upon Jesus is to see the character and intentions of the eternal God perfectly reflected or represented. And Jesus himself claims that if his disciples have seen him, they have seen the Father (John 14:9). They need look nowhere else. Such is their unity of person and purpose that Jesus reveals God to us. He does this in a supremely unique way. No doubt John Vincent Taylor had an eye on this truth in cleverly titling his memorable book on God, *The Christlike God*.[19] Karl Barth understandably speaks of Jesus in this context as the revealer: 'Everything else pales beside the fact that in him God is in the broadest sense speech, address, the Word that comes to us.' Similarly, Andrew Mayes, more recently, speaks of him as principally the revealer.[20] And, significantly, John the Baptist is witness to this revelation personified in the man, Jesus, 'He came as a witness… so that through him all might believe' (John 1:7).

It's worth mentioning briefly and as an aside that there is actually more revelation to come. Though this will always accord with the Lord's salvific purposes in Christ and with the scriptural narrative, it has not come to an end for us. If that were not the case, we would no doubt be perfect! In fact, we expect and, with Paul, pray for greater understanding and knowledge of God and his ways; the apostle prays for the Ephesians to be given 'the Spirit of wisdom and revelation' so that they might know God better (Ephesians 1:17). That's part of the dynamic and charismatic nature of the church, where individuals bring hymns, words of instruction, revelations, spiritual tongues and interpretation in order to build up and edify the church of Christ (1 Corinthians 14:26). Certainly, when we finally and gloriously see the Lord face-to-face, when we see Jesus 'as he is' (1 John 3:2), we'll realise only too unambiguously how distorted our reflected, dim-mirrored sight has been, despite our presently claimed certainties (1 Corinthians 13:12).

The Bible and revelation

Revelation and scripture are often thought of as synonymous, though in reality they are not. From what we've already seen, they are clearly and closely related, but they are not identical. As Larry Hart puts it, 'The Bible is not the Exodus; it is the inspired record of the Exodus.'[21] In simplistic terms, we might say that the revelation of God in word and deed to Israel inspired and produced the Old Testament. Similarly, the revelation of God in word and deed in Jesus Christ inspired and produced the New Testament. In that way, revelation preceded the Bible; the Bible is the written consequence of divine revelation. But they are not synonymous. Historical events, myth, divine words of instruction and command, visions and dreams; God's wrestling, passing by a prophet in a mountainous cleft, defeating enemies and punishing and redeeming faithless Israel; God's coming in Jesus Christ, miracles, parables, death by crucifixion, and glorious and vindicating resurrection – these are divine revelation. It is salutary to realise that they may have gone entirely unknown[22] had not God's Holy Spirit inspired writers and storytellers to recount them, to preserve them and to theologise on their meaning and significance, but in their original historical context they would still have revealed something of God and of his ways to those involved – both to Israel and the nations around them and to the church itself.

Revelation of God is only partial, of course; but it is, in Martin Luther's words, reliable and adequate. We've seen that in its developed sense revelation does not mean merely the transmission of a body of knowledge, of statements about God and his ways, but the personal disclosure of a gracious God in history – a God whose mission is to seek worshippers in the world (John 4:23). The Swiss theologian Emil Brunner is rightly adamant that revelation is not just about propositions, about truth-statements: 'Revelation is never the mere communication of knowledge, but a life-giving and life-renewing fellowship.' He continues, 'The self-revelation of God is not of an object… but a Person. A Person who is revealing himself, a Person who demands and offers Lordship and fellowship with himself.'[23] This is worth remembering as we read the Bible and is something to which we'll need to return.

Witness

The Bible, then, is a post-fall witness to God's revelation of himself, of his presence, intentions and historical activity. As such, it points to something other than itself, as do all created things, in that they all point to their creator. For instance, the apostle Paul speaks of creation itself revealing something of God, 'his eternal power and divine nature'. Paradoxically, these 'invisible qualities' are clearly seen, says Paul, 'being understood from what has been made' (Romans 1:20). The psalmist says as much in the poetry of Psalm 19:

> The heavens *declare* the glory of God;
>   the skies *proclaim* the work of his hands.
> Day after day they *pour forth* speech;
>   night after night they *display* knowledge.
> PSALM 19:1–2 (italics added)

The italicised words indicate the revelatory activity of the skies and the heavens; though they are devoid of words and sound (v. 3), they declare, proclaim, pour forth and display something of the God who brought them into being and sustains them. They witness to God's being and purpose, his glory and continuing creative occupation, his governing and preserving. He is God and there is no other.

Similarly, Israel itself was called and separated from the nations to be a witness of the uniqueness of God and his saving purposes for the world. There are several Old Testament passages that speak of this, but Isaiah 43 contains an adamant and clear statement:

> 'You are my witnesses,' declares the Lord,
> 'and my servant whom I have chosen,
> so that you may know and believe me
> and understand that I am he.'
>
> ISAIAH 43:10

Then, a little later, the Lord underlines the fact that he and no other has saved them.

> 'I have revealed and saved and proclaimed –
> I, and not some foreign god among you.
> You are my witnesses,' declares the Lord, 'that I am God.
> Yes, and from ancient days I am he.
> No-one can deliver out of my hand.
> When I act, who can reverse it?'
>
> ISAIAH 43:12–13

That which is revealed about God (his uniqueness, his faithfulness and the salvation that comes from his gracious activity in history) is to be witnessed to by Israel – that is the task for which they have been chosen and set apart. It's worth noticing, too, that the Lord takes the initiative through Israel; that is, they witness to his presence, but it is the Lord who displays his splendour *through them*. The prophet makes this clear where the Lord says, 'You are my servant, Israel, in whom I will display my splendour' (Isaiah 49:3).

Even the nations around Israel, nations that don't ostensibly recognise God for who he is, are called upon to be witnesses of the Lord's chastisement of his own people: 'Therefore hear, you nations,' says the prophet Jeremiah, 'you who are witnesses, observe what will happen to them' (Jeremiah 6:18).

The New Testament seems consciously to take up this theme of witnessing to the Lord's presence and purposes. John the Baptist, for example, is a man 'sent from God', coming as 'a witness to testify concerning that light, so that through him all might believe' (John

1:6–7). This is repeated to emphasise the designated calling: 'He himself was not the light; he came only as a witness to the light' (v. 8; see v. 15). In this context, Karl Barth appropriately speaks of John as 'the human witness who stands between revelation and humanity'.[24] John, the author of the gospel and letters, speaks in a similar vein about his authorial role:

> That which was from the beginning, which we have heard, which we have seen with our eyes, which we have looked at and our hands have touched – this *we proclaim* concerning the Word of life. The life appeared; we have seen it *and testify to it*, and *we proclaim* to you the eternal life… *We proclaim* to you what we have seen and heard.
> 1 JOHN 1:1–3 (italics added)

Again, the italicised words – together with the sense of physicality and of the very real presence of Jesus Christ, the Word of life – underlines the writer's awareness of his calling as a witness to God, to Jesus Christ and to the fellowship the Lord seeks of humanity: 'And our fellowship is with the Father and with his Son, Jesus Christ,' John continues (1 John 1:3). This is in line with Jesus' own words to the disciples, the nascent church, 'You will receive power when the Holy Spirit comes on you; and you will be my witnesses' (Acts 1:8). That testimonial work ostensibly begins at Pentecost (Acts 2).

However, the final and definitive witness to divine love is Jesus Christ himself, through whom God speaks (Hebrews 1:1–3). It's fascinating, too, that Jesus speaks of himself as a witness to his truth and that the Father in heaven witnesses to it as well: 'I am one who testifies for myself; my other witness is the Father, who sent me' (John 8:18).

The Bible, then, seems to fit into this whole context of being a witness to God and the divine purpose in his Son, Jesus Christ. The Bible is a continuing, written witness to how the Lord has revealed himself to the world; the Bible is a witness to that revelation. In

Larry Hart's words, 'Scripture preserves and communicates divine revelation.'[25] It speaks to us about God. It declares that God has spoken words of grace over a sinful and needy world. However, as a post-fallen, created sacrament or engine, it is neither inerrant nor definitive – only God has these characteristics. But it *is* reliable and has something of the authority of the Holy Spirit about it.

We might sum this section up in the words of Clark Pinnock and Robert Brow, words that echo what we've been saying:

> *Revelation*, then, does not refer to the Bible in the first instance but to God's revelation in history. Yet we would not know much about that revelation were it not for the biblical witnesses. Through their testimony, human though it is, the Spirit brings about true knowledge of God.[26]

2

The Holy Spirit and the Bible

We might outline two ways in which the Holy Spirit is involved in the authority of the Bible. First, adapting a scheme suggested by Stephen Fowl in his excellent book *Theological Interpretation of Scripture*,[27] we can see that the Holy Spirit is intimately involved in the sphere of providence surrounding the creation of the Christian scriptures. Fowl suggests that John's gospel gives us the clue to this. Consider the following outline in the context of the formation of the canon of scripture.

John 14:16	Jesus promises the Spirit of truth to his disciples.
John 14:26	The Spirit will teach the disciples the truth of Jesus.
John 14:26	The Spirit will remind the disciples what Jesus said and taught.
John 15:1–11	The Spirit will guide and direct the disciples concerning what is to come so that they can continue to abide in Christ.
John 16:13	The Spirit will guide them into 'all the truth'.
John 16:13	The Spirit will speak about the future.
John 16:14–15	The Spirit will gain what he relates to the disciples from Jesus himself.

The Holy Spirit is intimately involved in every aspect. Fowl writes, 'The Spirit's work in the operation of God's providential ordering of things sanctifies the means and processes that lead to the production of Scripture, turning them to God's holy purposes without diminishing their human, historical character.'[28]

Second, the Holy Spirit confirms to us that the scriptures witness to the truth of God. John Calvin, the 16th-century French reformer, speaks in this context of 'the inner witness of the Spirit' – the deep inner conviction that scripture is from God; that as we read the text of the Bible the Spirit affirms its own authenticity; that this book somehow faithfully witnesses the gracious revelation of God. Similarly, the Canadian Baptist theologian Stanley Grenz speaks of the Holy Spirit as the great 'Addresser', who speaks through the pages of the Bible: 'He is God's voice confronting us through Scripture. As such, he is the personal presence of God encountering us through God's own word.'[29] And again, Karl Rahner says that the Holy Spirit helps us to hear the word of God.[30] Scripture is what it says it is – God's word. It draws us into personal and empowering relationship with God, through Jesus Christ, by the energetic action of the Holy Spirit revealing God in Christ to us as well as our need of him and the purposes of God for our lives. And that summary statement brings us to the important question: why do we read the Bible?

3

Why do we read the Bible?

The apostle Paul sums up the goal of his own life in the extraordinarily simple yet powerful phrase, 'I want to know Christ' (Philippians 3:10). He clearly means more than knowing *about* Jesus, for he goes on to say that he wants 'to know the power of his resurrection and participation in his sufferings, becoming like him in his death, and so, somehow, attaining to the resurrection from the dead' (vv. 10–11). In this he has in mind his own spiritual identification with Jesus Christ and his gradual transformation into his image. Similarly, his goal for others is spelled out in his apostolic calling and purpose, 'We proclaim him [Jesus], admonishing and teaching everyone with all wisdom, so that we may present everyone fully mature in Christ' (Colossians 1:28).[31] So to know Christ, to be fully mature in Christ, to be transformed into the image of Christ – that is our personal aim, the goal of our lives and discipleship. It is important to see reading the Bible in that specific context, for scripture witnesses to us the revelation of God in Jesus Christ, and it leads us to oneness with him and maturity in him through the activity of the Holy Spirit.

As we have said, God's purpose in revealing himself to humanity is to connect with us in grace and to be involved with us, in order to save us – to have fellowship with us and us with him. To Jewish leaders who came to test Jesus, Jesus speaks this remarkable rebuke: 'You study the Scriptures diligently because you think that in them you possess eternal life. These are the very Scriptures that testify [witness] about me, yet you refuse to come to me to have life' (John 5:39–40). It seems that these leaders read the scriptures, but they didn't find eternal life, life with God, because they were not reading to find the Lord himself – and this, says Jesus, is the key to reading them: to find life in a relationship with Jesus Christ. So we read scripture to hear God speak to us, to relate to us in and through Christ.

Several contemporary Christian writers are very strong on this, none more so than Eugene Peterson. In an early work, *Working the Angles: The shape of pastoral integrity*, he says that 'the Christian's interest in the Scriptures has always been hearing God speak'.[32] He then usefully differentiates between reading the Bible and listening to it; we might say the difference between reading and engaging with it: 'In reading I open the book and attend to the words. I can read by myself; I cannot listen by myself. In listening the speaker is in charge, in reading the reader is in charge.'[33] We soon discover that the Bible has a voice 'directed to the reader-become-listener'[34] – God speaks to those who read the Bible in this way.

For some years now, I've read the Bible every twelve months or so. Beginning with the Psalms, I read the rest in a certain order, in lengthy portions, getting to know what the book is about. This, in itself, is useful, of course. However, this is what Eugene Peterson would term 'reading', not 'listening'. It's a good thing to do, but, as we've seen, it won't gain the desired purpose of scripture, which is for us to become mature in Christ, to know him in resurrection power and in suffering. To listen, I need to pause and contemplate the text, to pray through it, to reflect on the experience of God – Israel's or the writer's and my own – seeking to see the words as enculturated in the period of their composition but, somehow, through the wonderful present work of the Holy Spirit, applied to my own time and situation. To listen to scripture, I need to grasp something of the central importance of Jesus Christ to the narrative and to my own life and well-being; I need to grasp the importance of experiencing God through the Spirit as he informs my thinking and forms my life to exhibit something of Christ himself. It happens on a different level than merely reading scripture; it is 'listening to', or 'engaging with', scripture.

In his later work on the subject, *Eat This Book*, Eugene Peterson speaks of God revealing himself to us through the text of scripture as we 'listen', pulling us into the revelation and welcoming us as participants in it: 'God's word is written, handed down, and translated for us so that we can enter the plot.'[35] This is an important point. It perhaps reminds us of the active word in Peter Phillips' image of the Bible as an engine – an engine driving us to recognise the God behind the words.[36] But Peterson is speaking about the narrative of scripture, the story of God's people throughout biblical history (Old Testament and New), into which we are drawn by God's revelation to us through the witness of scripture. It reminds me of a fascinating study of tradition by Delwin Brown. Speaking of the curatorial character of tradition, he says it has force; it's experienced as some kind of distinctive pull. Employing an image, Brown speaks of it as more like a galaxy than a planet. The planet, he says, is static in its 'brute given-ness'; the galaxy, in contrast, functionally exerts its own gravitational pull, 'a kind of inner drive', with its ragged edges and its inner swirl.[37] This seems reminiscent of much of what Peterson says about biblical narrative. If we 'listen' to it, it pulls us in; it has its own gravitational pull, 'a kind of inner drive'. And, as we enter the narrative of scripture, we work out who we are, our roots; we negotiate our own identity – it's a very personal thing.

It's a personal experience because it involves primarily the God of revelation and us, those who listen to or engage with his compelling voice. Eugene Peterson helpfully puts it this way:

> But here's the thing: every aspect, every form is *personal* – God is relational at the core – and so whatever is said, whatever is revealed, whatever is received is also personal and relational… The corollary to this is that I, because I am a person, am personally involved in the revelation. Every word

I hear, everything I see in my imagination as the story unfolds, involves me relationally, pulls me into participation, *matters* to my core identity, affects who I am and what I do.[38]

Why read the Bible? Because in reading, or rather 'listening', to use Peterson's helpful distinction, we hear God's voice and discover his revelation to which the Bible is a faithful witness. We do so through other people's experiences of God and his salvation, and sometimes through their experiences of God's apparent absence. So it's not always going to be easy reading/listening! Indeed, at times it is difficult to glean the Lord's voice at all. But we read in the hope and the confidence that because he is personal, his purpose for us is good. We read so that we might enter the storyline or narrative plot and be transformed little by little into the image of his precious Son. We need to keep this in mind as we turn later to some strategies for reading the pages of scripture; we don't want to learn to read, only to miss the divine art and purpose of listening.

4

Biblical statements on scripture

Biblical writers sometimes speak of the nature of scripture, though they are not as clear as perhaps we'd wish them to be. Before moving to some macro-strategies on reading the Bible's narrative, we need to look at some of the more important New Testament texts on scripture.

2 Timothy 3:15–17

> … the Holy Scriptures, which are able to make you wise for salvation through faith in Christ Jesus. All Scripture is God-breathed and is useful for teaching, rebuking, correcting and training in righteousness, so that all God's people may be thoroughly equipped for every good work.

It is noteworthy that Paul's purpose is to explain the usefulness of scripture, not necessarily its nature. This isn't part of a systematic theology, but a letter to a spiritual protégé and young church leader. The apostle encourages Timothy to continue in what he's learned from his grandmother Lois and mother Eunice (2 Timothy 1:5), because the scriptures are able to make him wise for salvation.

Paul uses a unique term here, which the TNIV translates 'Holy Scriptures'. It could equally be translated 'sacred writings', but it clearly refers to the Old Testament, either parts of it or the whole.

These, he says, have been 'God-breathed', an image reminiscent of God breathing into Adam at creation (Genesis 2:7) or into the dry, lifeless bones in Ezekiel's graphic prophecy (Ezekiel 37:5). In both cases the Lord breathes into lifeless beings and brings them to life. Similarly, we might say, God brings the scriptures to life – they owe their distinctive character and purpose to the Spirit (breath) of God. It is because of this that scripture carries authority to transform people, to make them mature in faith. If we listen to the word, as Peterson suggests, we will be graciously taught, rebuked of our false beliefs, corrected in our behaviour and trained in righteousness.

2 Peter 1:20–21

Above all, you must understand that no prophecy of Scripture came about by the prophet's own interpretation of things. For prophecy never had its origin in the human will, but prophets, though human, spoke from God as they were carried along by the Holy Spirit.

Whereas Paul spoke about the inspiration of the scriptures, the apostle Peter speaks here of the inspiration of the writers. Peter seems to be defending the expectation of the second coming of Christ (the *parousia*) by reference to Old Testament prophecy (2 Peter 1:19), the authority of which his opponents appear to be rejecting.

Peter affirms that prophecy in the Old Testament had its origin in the revelatory will of God, that the prophets were borne along or impelled by the Spirit of God. Many commentators see this as a sailing metaphor. Michael Green, for instance, says that 'the prophets raised their sails… and the Holy Spirit filled them and carried them along in the direction he wished'.[39] Peter is not commending a dictation theory; he underlines the fact that prophecy comes from *both* God and human beings. The phrase 'carried along' gives a sense of 'enlivened', 'animated' – an image we discovered in Paul's understanding, too.

Acts 4:25

> You spoke by the Holy Spirit through the mouth of your servant,
> our father David:
> > 'Why do the heathens rage
> > and the peoples plot in vain?'

This prayer by the nascent church is addressed to God, the Father (Acts 4:27, 30). Though the Greek is extremely difficult here, the text probably refers to the mouth of David rather than referring to David as God's mouthpiece (as in the TNIV translation). By quoting Psalm 2 in the way they do, the disciples emphasise again that scripture (in this case the Psalms) originates both with the human writer, David, and with God – and that it is the Holy Spirit in particular who inspires the text. However, it is fascinating to see how the praying church uses the inspired words of scripture as a springboard, rather than as a static text. They quote Psalm 2, which concludes rather negatively with the words, 'Kiss the son, or he will be angry and you and your ways will be destroyed' (Psalm 2:12), but they pray that the Lord will enable them to speak the gospel 'with great boldness' (Acts 4:29), healing and demonstrating the power of God through miracles, signs and wonders – a prayer that is graciously answered throughout the history of the early church, retold by Luke in the book of Acts.

2 Peter 3:16

Speaking of Paul, Peter writes:

> He writes the same way in all his letters… His letters contain some things that are hard to understand, which ignorant and unstable people distort, as they do the other Scriptures, to their own destruction.

It is important to note that the word translated here as 'Scriptures' may be, and probably should be, translated 'writings', and that it evidently refers to the Old Testament, or at least to parts of it. This, then, is a remarkable verse, as it shows a growing awareness in the early church that some of their contemporary writings (in this case, Paul's pastoral letters) had the authority of the Holy Spirit himself – similar to those of the Old Testament. In other words, Peter is recognising that Paul's writing was being used by God to reveal himself and his gracious purposes in Jesus Christ. His letters were speaking to the people to whom they were written; they were transforming lives; they bear witness to God's acts in creating, sustaining, redeeming and completing his divine purpose; they bring life. The apostle's epistles are a witness to divine revelation.

Part II

Macro-strategies: how to read the narrative

It is very important at this point to emphasise that reading strategies do not replace a spiritual reading, a listening (in Eugene Peterson's word) to God through the scriptures, a faithful engagement with the Bible as a witness to divine revelation. George Müller (1805–98), an evangelist and a godly man of great practical faith, who established Christian orphanages in and around Bristol, said that he read scripture every morning and refused to get up from his knees before the Lord had spoken to him personally. That's the kind of Bible reading we want to aspire to: a faithful listening for the voice of God in a living encounter. So reading strategies, though immensely helpful, must never take the place of faith, prayer, spiritual engagement and waiting on the Lord. Following that disclaimer, let's look at one or two helpful Bible-reading strategies.

The first strategies – macro-strategies or big-picture strategies – look at the Bible as a whole, or more accurately at the biblical narrative. They are essentially thematic and allow us to place both the text of scripture and ourselves into the story of divine grace traced out in both testaments and beyond. They encourage us to pattern our lives around our core beliefs, while keeping God himself at the centre of our Bible reading.

5

The linear model: where are we in the narrative?

The biblical documents have always functioned in the Christian community as both forming and informing canon. One way they do this is through paradigmatic themes or events – experiences that Israel or the church have been through which take on the function of a crucial and explanatory pattern for faith and life in relationship with God. Creation,[40] the flood (e.g. Isaiah 54:9), the exodus,[41] Passover,[42] resurrection (e.g. 2 Corinthians 1:9) and other motifs gain a regulative function as the images are repeated throughout the tradition and experienced in new and Spirit-determined ways. This establishes both identity and continuity with the past. Israel, standing at a moral crossroads, is encouraged to 'ask for the ancient paths, ask where the good way is, and walk in it' (Jeremiah 6:16). By joining the narrative, 'the ancient paths', by being pulled into it, people of faith such as ourselves have creatively reconstructed inherited symbols and paradigms – 'the construction of a tradition's future from the resources of its past'.[43]

What, then, are the major coordinates of the biblical narrative? Christopher Wright suggests they are: creation, the fall, redemption and the new creation.[44] This linear model is illustrated in the following diagram.

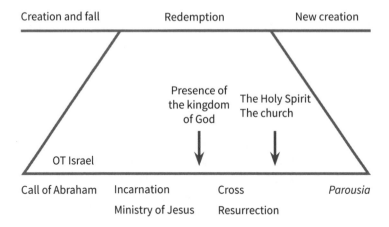

Creation and fall   Redemption   New creation

Presence of the kingdom of God   The Holy Spirit / The church

OT Israel

Call of Abraham   Incarnation   Cross   *Parousia*
                    Ministry of Jesus   Resurrection

Notice across the top line, from left to right, the four coordinates that Wright suggests: creation, the fall, redemption and the new creation. This is the biblical story, from beginning to end, from the origins of life in the creation of the world and of living things to the consummation of the divine purposes at the *parousia* (the second coming) of Jesus Christ in glory and the establishment of the new creation (Revelation 21—22). Notice, importantly, that this line takes us beyond the confines of the Bible itself in the sense that we find ourselves on that line. We are there after the Christ-event ('history's hinge', as Terry Hinks graphically calls it),[45] but previous to his return. It might help at this point to place yourself on that line in the diagram. See yourself there. We'll come back to that a little later.

The bottom of the two parallel lines expands on or magnifies the redemption coordinate in some more detail. It's as if we're putting a magnifying glass up to the word 'redemption' on the top line. Here it is in a slightly more detailed way. We haven't space to elaborate on this, nor is it the purpose of this book, but a brief recount should suffice.

Redemption in history begins with the call of and the divine promises to Abram (Genesis 12:1-3), graphically repeated in God's covenant with him in Genesis 15. Further to this, the miraculous release of the Israelites from Egypt (Exodus 12—14) and the giving of the law on Mount Sinai (Exodus 19—20:21) continue the theme and narrative of divine redemption as it is applied to the people of Israel, who are called to be God's chosen people and witnesses of divine presence and redemptive revelation. Moving along the storyline, towards the right, Israel largely fails to show God's redemptive purposes for the world, so the Lord judges them, punishing the people with exile from the promised land. Generations later, God sends his Son, Jesus Christ, to be not only Israel's redeemer but also the Saviour of the whole world (John 1:29), continuing the theme of divine redemption for which Abram and Israel were graciously called. After Jesus' death, resurrection and ascension, the church is called upon to be the witness of the redeeming presence of God in the world. To aid them in this the Lord fills them with the Holy Spirit at Pentecost and beyond, giving them (and us?) courage and the ability to speak the good news of the gospel to a needy world and to demonstrate the kingdom of God through acts of mercy and miracles of healing and the like. Finally, at the *parousia* all creation will be redeemed, reconciled to God through Jesus Christ.

That is much too brief and inadequate a summary of the Bible's story, but it might give a sense of the narrative flow of that redemption coordinate that Christopher Wright indicates.[46] Now, let's look at the four coordinates from a slightly different angle.

Creation

As you can imagine, creation gives us our foundational principles. If you like, it shows the *ideals* of God's creation. What are those ideals, the principles that are laid down at this point in the biblical narrative? Foremost among these are the truths about God himself that creation teaches us. He is sovereign, powerful, creative, imaginative, outgoing, relational and loving, and his purposes are entirely inclusive. The biblical teaching on creation underlines the fact that there is only one God; there is no other. We can see this working out as the biblical writers contemplate what it means for God to be the creator. For example, the writer of 1 Chronicles reaches this conclusion: 'For the gods of the nations are idols, but the Lord made the heavens' (1 Chronicles 16:26). Jeremiah is adamant about this connection: 'But the Lord is the true God; he is the living God, the eternal King… These gods, who did not make the heavens and the earth, will perish… But God made the earth by his power' (Jeremiah 10:10–12). Divine creating indicates that God is in control (Jeremiah 27:4–5) and that he can be trusted in his ability to do anything (Jeremiah 32:17). Creation itself is ordered, beautiful, good, contingent upon God and diverse, and it reflects the glory of its divine maker and sustainer. Humanity is unique, made in the image of God, accountable, dependent on each other and upon God, relational, free and good. Men and women are complementary and equal. What else does the creation show us? How would you add to this short list? Remember, these indicate God's ideals for his world.

The fall

The fall (Genesis 3) indicates the *realism* of the current, contemporary situation: disobedience, sin, pride, seeking after independence, relationships fractured, antagonism, vulnerability, disease, suffering, death, spiritual blindness and lies. How would you add to this pretty negative list? Remember, though, that the ideals (though in a broken and fragile manner) still underpin the situation. We mustn't allow the realism of the present circumstances to overshadow the continuing grace of God, who sees us and is mindful of us day upon day (Psalm 8). We still bear the image of God, though it is distorted, perhaps. Like a perfect mosaic nudged from one side – the pieces pushed, the picture out of shape – so are we post-fall. However, there is something noble, though broken, about humanity; there is undoubtedly beauty in a fallen world.

Redemption

God, in love, chose neither to abandon nor to destroy his creation. Though Genesis 3 strongly implies this (see Genesis 3:21–24, for example), a later episode makes this abundantly clear. In the narrative of Noah and the flood we see that God's original creational intentions for humanity are reasserted through a covenant with Noah (Genesis 6:18), a covenant echoing the original creational ordinance with Adam and Eve, a covenant that includes Noah's family, the earth and every living thing – just as at the beginning. And immediately following the flood, though the Lord sees that humanity will not change (8:21), he reasserts again the covenant with Noah (9:9), giving him 'everything' (9:3) and promising never to destroy the earth again (9:15–16). The Old Testament scholar Walter Brueggemann rightly claims that it is God's deep grief that distinguishes God from every other god and creature. But despite this grief, he affirms, 'God yields no ground on his purpose for creation.'[47] In redemption *he reasserts the ideals* in a fallen world. In fact, says Brueggemann, 'If anything, this is an even more exalted view of humanity.'[48]

Through Abram (later Abraham) God promises universal grace and salvation, re-establishing that promise in his covenant with Israel, as we've already noted. In Jesus Christ the kingdom of God is inaugurated; through his death and resurrection, evil is overcome and the Spirit is given. In the church, his people, the ideals of creation are reasserted – relationships are made whole, cultural and racial rivalry is done away with (e.g. Ephesians 2:11–22), societal, gender and ethnic differences are excluded (e.g. Galatians 3:28), and so on. That is, in the New Testament, we see a new creation coming into being. Jesus' life and teachings exemplify this new creation, the ideals of God in the flesh (the incarnational principle).

The church, too, is supposed to embody these foundational ideals; it has a glimpse of them. At its best, it seeks to live by them through the sanctifying work of the Spirit, but in this fallen world we are bound to continue to be both justified *and* sinful (in Martin Luther's words). We know with the apostle Paul that in our minds we are slaves to God's law but in our sinful nature we are slaves to the law of sin (Romans 7:22–23). Fascinatingly, the apostle questions who would rescue him from the present ambivalent situation, answering, 'Thanks be to God, who delivers me through Jesus Christ our Lord' (Romans 7:25). The next section draws upon that deliverance.

The new creation

The new creation at the second coming of Jesus Christ will *re-establish the ideals* of God. In fact, it will do that and much more. It's not merely about returning to the garden of Eden, nor about a simple repristination. After all, Jesus Christ has come. The Holy Spirit has indwelt the church. One day, says the prophet Isaiah, 'the earth will be filled with the knowledge of the Lord as the waters cover the sea' (Isaiah 11:9). John on Patmos remarks that a time is coming when death, tears, pain, suffering and mourning will be no more (Revelation 21:4), when the nations will walk by the light of God (21:24), when there will be no more curse (22:3) and when we will see God's face and will reign with him forever and ever (22:4–5). The apocalyptic Christ exclaims, 'I am making everything new!' (21:5).

What a narrative! From good creation to new creation; from humanity walking in the garden with the living God to the whole world seeing God face-to-face, seeing him 'as he is' (1 John 3:2).

Christopher Wright outlines the benefits of this linear model:

- It is canonical; it respects the shape and structure of the whole Bible. It does this because it takes seriously the biblical narrative.
- It is comprehensive in that it makes use of the whole Bible, from beginning to end, including both the Old and the New Testaments.
- It is community-oriented, centring as it does on the divine covenant with humanity through Abraham, through Israel and ultimately through Jesus Christ.

- It is contemporary. As I've pointed out, we stand on that line; we are there in the dynamic and progress of the biblical story of divine history.

At Center Parcs, there is what is known as 'the rapids'. It is basically a slide that travels around the main building, inside and out, with water rushing along it, down steep sections, over waterfalls, through flowing pools, and so on. To enter this experience, you have to clamber over a wall that takes you from a static pool to the beginning of the rapid water slide. Once you enter, though, you are quickly taken by the flowing water and by the people already in the rapids along its whole length. Try as you may, you have to keep moving forward; water and other swimmers carry and push you along until, at the end, you reach the finish – a small standing pool – tired but exhilarated.

Similarly, by faith and the Holy Spirit, by fellow believers and experience, we are pulled into the biblical narrative as we read and listen to the scriptures. Many have gone before us. Many travel with us. But there is a dynamic about this, which is picked up by the linear model. We are on the line. History moves on. There is a dynamic movement to salvation history and biblical narrative. We might draw an arrow pointing to the right on the top line of the diagram to indicate that history is being drawn inexorably by divine grace – history, and us with it.

The linear model helps us to read scripture because it allows us to see the whole sweep of redemptive history – past, present and future. It enables us to fit passages of scripture into that history, and this will encourage us to be realistic about what we read. For example, in reading about slavery, we'll realise that the Old Testament is not definitive. It doesn't tell us all we need to know. We know there is something more wholesome as the Lord seeks to reassert ideals through the life and teaching of Jesus and later through the life of the church (e.g. Ephesians 6:5–9; Philemon). Similarly, when we read the misogynist and patriarchal comments of the Old Testament, we will reckon on both the original intention (the ideals) of equality (Genesis 1:27) and the re-establishment of them in and through the church (Galatians 3:28).

Sadly, because of fallenness and sin, we don't completely regain those creational ideals in this period, but we notice that the apostle Paul, for example, is pushing, straining towards them in his injunctions to the church. Looking at the example of misogyny, he makes sure that the relationship between husband and wife is reciprocal ('Submit to one another out of reverence to Christ', Ephesians 5:21), that the husband is accountable too ('Love your wives, just as Christ loved the church and gave himself up for her', 5:25) and that relationships are experienced under the lordship of Christ in an entirely spiritual context (Ephesians 5:21, 22–25, 29). It took future generations (both Christians and others) to ban slavery in England, for example. But, from this model which indicates a historical progression, we would expect that.

See for yourself

Take a theme that interests you and trace it through the whole Bible using the linear model. You might like to use a concordance or a website, such as **biblegateway.com**. Short concordances are often found at the back of Bibles today.

The theme of God's presence is a good one to start with – tracing his direct, unmediated presence in the garden of Eden and comparing that with his self-revelation in the tabernacle and the temple, through priests, prophets and then uniquely in Jesus Christ, God made flesh, and in the church. Finally, you'll notice his presence in the new creation. Which passages have you employed? Where on the linear model are they to be found? How do they compare? How are they different? Do they illustrate the linear model's emphasis on the foundational ideals being reasserted, and re-established through history? How pivotal is Jesus in this progression (see John 1:14,

'The Word became flesh and made his dwelling among us')? How important is the church in all of this (see 1 Corinthians 3:16, 'You yourselves are God's temple... God's Spirit dwells among you'; 2 Corinthians 6:16, 'For we are the temple of the living God')?

Alternatively, when you come to something that intrigues you in a biblical passage – for example, law, election, covenant, war, Israel, the other nations, idols, divorce or spiritual freedom – trace it through the progressive revelation of the scriptures, teasing out the ideals and exploring these in the life of Jesus and his church. You may also like to go beyond the biblical narrative. Has history or society revealed anything on this theme? What about the church today? How will this be demonstrated in the new heavens and the new earth in which dwells righteousness?

Doing these exercises, you'll realise how significant creation and the new creation are to our understanding.

These exercises could be undertaken by a group. Each person could start at a different place in the narrative, exploring the topic under one of the headings: creation, fall, redemption and new creation. Examine what the Bible says at that point, ask why it is as it is and then come back together, fitting the pieces into a whole narrative timeline.

The table on the facing page gives a brief and incomplete outline for the subject of marriage as it's depicted through the biblical narrative. This is just the start of your exploration. Tease out the meaning of each passage within the context in which it appears in the biblical narrative. Attempt to find other passages that relate to the subject. Ask what the *purpose* of each text is. Can you see any progression as the story unfolds? And, remembering that we are on the line, or in the narrative, ask what this means to us today as we grapple with contemporary questions on this crucial subject. How do we define marriage? Does the biblical account allow for alternatives to the traditional view? Can we say that there is a biblical view of

Coordinate	Bible passage	Comment
Creation	Genesis 1:26–27	Both together in the image of God
	Genesis 2	A suitable helper, one flesh
Fall	Genesis 3	Adam names Eve; the Lord clothes them
Redemption	Deuteronomy 24:1–4	'A certificate of divorce'
	Deuteronomy 24:5	A newly married soldier stays home to 'bring happiness to the wife he has married'
	Malachi 2:16	God 'hates divorce'
	Matthew 19	Jesus' use of the creation ideals
	Ephesians 5:21–33	Submit to one another
	Galatians 3:28	There is neither male nor female, for all are one in Christ
New creation	Luke 20:35	No marriage in heaven for 'those who are considered worthy of taking part in the age to come'
	Revelation 21—22	What does this say about the topic?

marriage? What is the essence of the institution of marriage? Why is God involved in it? Is it a creational ordinance or a covenantal one? And many more questions could be asked at this point.

This is a model rich in potential. Using it in this way will develop an individual's or a group's method of reading the Bible, of engaging with its narrative and listening to its voice. One clear problem with it, however, is that we need to know our way both around the biblical narrative and around the Bible, 'the Bible as an actual book'.[49] But that will come in time if you keep reading it.

6

The triangular model: how do the Old and New Testaments fit together?

The Bible has two parts, the Old Testament and the New Testament, and the relationship between these two testaments has always intrigued Christians, because the two parts are believed to form a single narrative. The triangular model is useful when we're looking at this relationship. The model starts with the creational triangle, representing the beginning of the long narrative, and it extends to take into account both the Old Testament and the New. Here is the creational triangle.

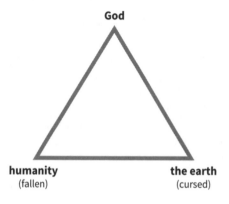

God

humanity
(fallen)

the earth
(cursed)

You'll notice that at the apex of the creational triangle (and each recurring triangle as we go on) is God. He is the constant in a changing story. This creational triangle equates to the first coordinate of the linear model we looked at earlier. As God creates, he forms a relationship with both humanity and the earth.

We notice that in the creation account, the earth is formed for humanity; the climax of divine activity is the creation of Adam and Eve, man and woman, together formed in the image of the living God (Genesis 1:26–27). Wolfhart Pannenberg is rightly adamant about this: 'God's creative action is oriented wholly to creatures. They are both the object and the goal of creation.' He speaks of creation as 'an expression of God's love'.[50] The psalmist, meditating on the Lord creating the heavens, tells us that God made us a little lower than himself (Psalm 8:5).

So the triangle represents a dynamic creation relationship – a three-way relationship, with the earth included with humanity and vital in God's continuing creative plans. In a parallel passage that underscores this, the Lord re-establishes his covenant with Noah by setting a rainbow in the clouds, 'the sign of the covenant between me and the earth... between me and you and all living creatures of every kind' (Genesis 9:13, 15).

This first triangle reminds us that originally God established a relationship with humanity and the earth. But we notice, too, that the relationship has fractured – humanity is fallen, the earth is cursed (see Genesis 3). That profound comment is the equivalent of the second coordinate of the linear model – the fall. Though the relationship is retained, the situation is made radically different through the entrance of disobedience and sin.

The second triangle indicates that God in grace establishes a narrower, more focused relationship, this time with Israel and the land. The people of Israel now inhabit the promised land, which in itself becomes a crucial part of the divine covenant. 'See, I have given you this land,' the Lord says. 'Go in and take possession of the land that the Lord swore he would give to your fathers – to Abraham, Isaac and Jacob – and to their descendants after them' (Deuteronomy 1:8). The land has been divinely promised to Israel; it becomes vital to their faith and being: 'Trust in the Lord and do good,' says the psalmist, 'dwell in the land and enjoy safe pasture' (Psalm 37:3).

This is why the loss of the land because of Judah's disobedience is so telling, so poignant. The prophecy of Jeremiah concludes with the exile; notice how it's stated: 'So Judah went into captivity, away from her land' (Jeremiah 52:27). The land represents the covenant promises of and fellowship with their God. However, the first creational triangle and its envisaged relationships are still very much in sight as the Lord calls Israel to occupy the land *in order* to witness to the being, oneness, grace and redemption of God:

'You are my witnesses,' declares the Lord,
   'and my servant whom I have chosen.'
ISAIAH 43:10 (see also 43:12)

This second triangle basically represents the Old Testament, or more specifically the coordinate of redemption in the linear model. It demonstrates God's purposes for Israel – purposes that they largely failed to fulfil.

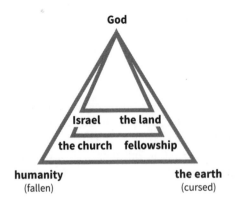

You'll notice that the base of the third triangle is wider than the second with the new covenant made between God and the universal church, inclusive of people of all languages and nationalities. We're reminded here that through Jesus Christ the divisions that plague fallen humanity are broken down – 'There is neither Jew nor Gentile, neither slave nor free, neither male nor female, for you are all one in Christ Jesus' (Galatians 3:28; see also Ephesians 2:11–22).

You may wonder why the bottom right-hand corner of the triangle is labelled 'fellowship'. Previously, we've had 'earth' and 'land', two rather more physical, tangible things. The thought here is that this is what we all share now in the new covenant, the church age. We don't now share the physical land as Israel once did. We share fellowship –

that is, the tangible manifestation of what it means to be the church. This is illustrated in the early church in Acts, for example, where 'they devoted themselves to the apostles' teaching and to fellowship, to the breaking of bread and to prayer' (Acts 2:42; see also Acts 4:32). Paul surely alludes to this fellowship in the following passage from his letter to the Philippian church:

> Therefore, if you have any encouragement from being united with Christ, if any comfort from his love, if any common sharing in the Spirit, if any tenderness and compassion, then make my joy complete by being like-minded, having the same love, being one in spirit and of one mind.
> PHILIPPIANS 2:1–2

The word 'if' here is a word of certainty, not questioning or doubt. The apostle uses the same form when he says, 'If God is for us, who can be against us? (Romans 8:31) – not suggesting for a minute that God is not for them. So here, in Philippians, he might have said, 'Because you have encouragement, because you have comfort, because you have a common sharing…' and so on. The apostle is reminding them of the encouragement, comfort, sharing, tenderness and compassion that they experience. He then exhorts them to fellowship together on this basis: 'Do nothing out of selfish ambition or vain conceit. Rather, in humility value others above yourselves, not looking to your own interests but each of you to the interests of the others' (Philippians 2:3–4). This is the fellowship we all share as Christians. Again, having witnessed to believers about the reality of Jesus' presence in the world, the apostle John gives his reason: 'We proclaim to you what we have seen and heard, so that you may also have fellowship with us. And our fellowship is with the Father and with his Son, Jesus Christ' (1 John 1:3). Fellowship is central to what it means to have relationship with God and with his people. We share that together as a Spirit-enlivened reflection of our fellowship with the Lord.

The final triangle takes us to the eschatological climax of God's purposes in Christ. Ultimately, humanity is redeemed and the Lord brings a new heaven and a new earth into being. Notice how this triangle re-establishes the first one – it encompasses the whole of humanity, not merely the nation of Israel ('the nations will walk by its light' – Revelation 21:24; see 22:2). The Hebrew prophet Isaiah seems to have grasped this truth. The Lord says through him that Israel will be made 'a light for the Gentiles', that his salvation will reach 'the ends of the earth' (Isaiah 49:6); indeed, that nations will come running to the splendour of Israel (55:5; see also Isaiah 52:10; 56:7). The new creation represents the perfect world restored, in which men and women live in righteousness together, from which all evil is excluded; it is, in fact, Eden restored – and much, much more. At that time all glory and praise will be given to the one, sovereign, covenant-keeping God. Every knee will bow and every mouth will acknowledge 'that Jesus Christ is Lord' (Philippians 2:11).

The triangular model is very useful indeed:

- In a similar way to the linear model, this has dynamic and movement in that it traces the purposes of God, formed in creation, through his repeated post-fall establishment of the creational relationship with Israel, with the church, with redeemed humanity. As you look at the final triangular model, you can discern this movement in a glance.

- The triangular model quite clearly follows the shape of the Old Testament and the New – you can visualise them as you look at the final figure.

- The triangular shape reflects the outward-going, expansive, missional nature of the task that the Lord entrusts to his people.

- Interestingly, we are on the base of two triangles. Not only are we on the church/fellowship line, but we also appear on the humanity (fallen)/the earth (cursed) one. That gives us both our task and our context. The former base establishes us in God's missional purposes for the church; the latter reminds us of our own and the world's fallenness, fragility and continual need of grace.

- Finally, the model also indicates the influence of paradigms – both themes and experiences – running through the Old Testament to the New (hence the top arrow pointing down) and the stimulus of eschatology impacting the way we read history and the way we behave (the arrow pointing up the triangles). The former runs down or forward through the narrative (see Isaiah 51:1–2); the latter pushes up or backwards, intruding the present time to influence present thought and discipleship.

Let's pause for a moment to see how this works. We've noticed above how experiences from Israel's past become paradigms for their present thought and conduct. A specific occurrence will teach the people of Israel something about the nature of God or of salvation, and that specific instance will become a general paradigm or a pattern for later. This is similar to my experience of learning French. For example, when I'd learned the specific conjugation of the French verb *finir* (to finish, to end, to complete), I could apply that to every single regular '-ir' verb in the French language. It became my paradigm for doing so. So, too, the Israelites learned that they could (and should) apply lessons learned in the past about the Lord and his ways to contemporary experiences.

As so often, Isaiah the prophet gives us a good example. He calls upon the people in the following way:

> Listen to me, you who pursue righteousness
>   and who seek the Lord:
> look to the rock from which you were cut
>   and to the quarry from which you were hewn;
> look to Abraham, your father,
>   and to Sarah, who gave you birth.
> When I called him he was only one man,
>   and I blessed him and made him many.
> ISAIAH 51:1–2

Isaiah calls upon Israel to consider a specific historical event – the birth of the people of God through God's gracious work in the lives of Abraham and Sarah long ago. But it's not just a past event; it becomes a paradigm for what the Lord is able to do today, for the prophet encourages them through the Lord's words, 'My salvation is on the way, and my arm will bring justice to the nations' (Isaiah 51:5). If universal salvation appears impossible for the Israelites in their current situation, then they need to look back at the miracle of Isaac's birth from a man who was 'as good as dead' (Hebrews 11:12) and realise not only that God is able to work powerfully in the world, but that he is also committed to his covenant. The thought becomes a paradigm, a fixed point of departure, an assurance, the very foundation of their theology of God.

Eschatology works the other way around. Rather than looking backwards to lessons learned from historical events, eschatology moves from the consummation, or from the heavenlies, and works its influential way into our thinking and discipleship. In this way, the Holy Spirit brings heaven to bear upon our contemporary lives. The apostle Paul gives us a clear example of this in his letter to the church in Colossae: 'Since, then, you have been raised with Christ, set your hearts on things above, where Christ is seated at the right hand of God. Set your minds on things above, not on earthly things' (Colossians 3:1–2). The consequence of this is not ethereal or insubstantial, as we might expect; instead it includes putting to death 'sexual immorality, impurity, lust, evil desires and greed' (3:5).[51]

We normally think of the biblical narrative as simply moving forward from creation to the new creation. But it is clear that the influence derives from both directions. The future claims present behaviour; it forms a sort of living template and dynamic of what the Lord requires. It's seen in the person of Jesus, the message he proclaimed, the life he lived and the kingdom he inaugurated.

So, though a little complex at this point, I hope you can see how helpful the triangular model is in reading the whole of scripture and in seeing its shape, its structure and where we sit in its narrative.

See for yourself

The book of Hebrews in the New Testament might be an appropriate place to start when considering the triangular model and its implications for reading the biblical text. This is because the author of the letter is very aware of the relationship between the Old and New Testaments in the narrative of the divine encounter and grace. Continually, he challenges his readers to compare the new story in Jesus Christ with that of the old. For example, he speaks of Jesus as being greater than Moses (Hebrews 3:1–19), of the present spiritual rest being better than the one given through Joshua (4:1–13, note particularly v. 8), of Jesus' high priesthood being more perfect and 'the source of eternal salvation for all who obey him' (5:1–10, particularly v. 8; 8:1–13), of the eternal worth of Jesus' sacrifice compared to those of the old covenant (9:1—10:18), of the holy mountain Zion in contrast to 'the mountain of fear', Mount Sinai (12:18–29), and so on.

Why not read this letter through the perspective of the triangular model? Read the letter through slowly and carefully, noting the times when the author mentions the Old Testament topics and compares them to the New Testament. You'll see how the instances from the Old Testament become paradigms for the New. When you've read the text, locate what the writer is speaking of in the Old Testament – for example, when he mentions Mount Sinai as a mountain of fear, darkness, gloom and storm, read Exodus 19, which recounts this formative event in the history of the people of God. Now, he says, we come to a different mountain, the city of the living God, the city of Zion. Ask:

- How does he compare the two?
- Does that help you to shape the history of God's people – the Israelites and the church?
- Does it give hints on how to read the relationship between the Old and New Testaments?
- And, most importantly, where does Jesus fit into this structure, this shape? (In fact, if you look carefully, you'll see that he is absolutely pivotal to the shape.)

Do the same exercise with other topics. Lastly, recall the shape of the triangular model. Does this shape help to interpret the biblical topic you've been looking at?

A second way you can see for yourself is to take some themes or topics from the Old Testament and try to work through the way in which they develop and morph into New Testament understanding.

You could take covenant, for example, or priesthood, worship, Israel or mission. The topic of war is a good one to look at, too, as that changes radically through the people's understanding both of God and of his missional purposes. When it resurfaces, for instance in Paul's letters (e.g. Ephesians 6:10–20), it becomes 'spiritualised' in the church's thinking. What does that say about the progress of the Bible's story – a progress that concludes in the war-torn pages of the book of Revelation?

7

The Bible as God's drama: Christian improvisation

We have seen repeatedly that the Bible's story, or narrative, is important if we are to read it well and engage with it. It isn't so much the story as story that is significant, but rather the actual living history into which we are invited or called by the Spirit of God. As we put our faith in God, as we trust and follow Jesus Christ and as we are filled with the Holy Spirit, we are drawn into the history of God's dealings with the world, the biblical history of Israel and the life of the early church and beyond. This is where our story is taken into the story of God, where we find our identity in Christ and his kingdom and where we are offered salvation. Story is important. We've seen this to be the case in both the linear and the triangular models. Story is important, too, if we look at the Bible, as some do, as an unfinished play script.

Some theologians suggest that the Bible is God's story, or God's drama (more technically, theodrama). The most prominent of these theologians are Tom Wright, a leading English New Testament scholar, based at the University of Oxford, and Kevin Vanhoozer, a systematic theologian in Trinity Evangelical Divinity School, following the lead of the significant Swiss theologian Hans Urs von Balthasar. While Wright divides the Bible's narrative into creation, the fall, Israel, Christ and the church, Vanhoozer lists it slightly differently: creation, Israel, Christ, Pentecost/church and the consummation.[52] The scheme that Vanhoozer suggests gives more prominence to the divine working in the story.

To examine and explore this strategy, let's take a step back for a moment and start at a slightly different place. Imagine that you're digging in the garden when your spade hits a different sounding object. You unearth the object with some anticipation, take it out and look carefully at what you've discovered. On examination, you realise that it's the manuscript of a very old play marvellously preserved – you recognise it as a play by William Shakespeare, as yet undiscovered. As you've always enjoyed the Bard's plays, you read this one with considerable interest, poring over each page and line, until you get to where the last act should be, only to find it missing.

Let's say the previously unknown play that you've dug up is *Romeo and Juliet*. However, all you've found under the earth is the first four acts and scene 1 of act 5. You read what you have, and you are determined to stage it anyway. The question at this point is how to go about staging a Shakespeare play with the vital last scenes missing.

Why don't you consider this question before moving on? What would you need to do to make your completed version as authentic as possible? Where would you start? Let me suggest a few pointers.

- First, you'd need a group of committed people interested and willing to take a part in the production of the to-be-extended play. You couldn't go solo on a project like this – just look at the list of characters, for example! So a small group, or *community*, is required.

- It would be good at the beginning of your discussion to have some Shakespeare *experts* in the group. Ideally, you'd like a Shakespeare scholar and researcher – perhaps the director of the Shakespeare Institute in Stratford. And why not, for good measure, a Shakespearean actor and director, like Sir Kenneth Branagh? With their considerable knowledge and expertise, they would direct your thinking and writing, your acting and conclusions.

- You'd need to keep the end of the play *consistent* with the part that you have. So you'd need to get to know the first four acts and act 5, scene 1, really well. You'd read them again and again, over and over until you felt sure you understood where it might be going, who the characters are, what their roles will be, how they relate and so on. Only in that way could you be anywhere near certain that your play will conclude in a genuinely Shakespearean manner, perhaps even close to how the playwright intended. What has been the character's role until this point? How would you expect them to respond to the narrative flow of the play?

- You'd read some more of Shakespeare's plays to get a feel of his writing, his language, his imagery, his characterisation, his plot twists and the like.

- In the case of *Romeo and Juliet*, you have the Prologue to guide you – in which the playwright gives you not only *explicit hints* about the story and characters (see the italicised words below) but also how long the play lasts ('two hours' traffic of our stage')!

  Two households, both alike in dignity,
  In fair Verona, where we lay our scene,
  From *ancient grudge* break new mutiny,
  and *civil blood* makes civil hands unclean.
  From forth *the fatal loins* of these two foes
  A pair of star-crossed lovers take their life;
  Whose misadventure'd piteous overthrows
  Doth with *their death* bury their parents' strife.
  The fearful passage of their *death-mark'd love*,
  And the continuance of their parents' rage,
  Which but their children's end nought could remove,
  Is now the two hours' traffic of our stage.[53]

- Your group would *discuss* a lot before concluding anything. You'd accept some interpretations; you'd reject others. You'd need to *compromise* in this discussion, too.

- Finally, you'd actually have to act that last part of the play. I imagine you'd improvise what you've previously thought through, then you'd discuss it. Sometimes that *improvisation* would work, you'd consider it right or appropriate. Sometimes, though, you wouldn't get the improvisation 'right' or good enough, and you'd have to go back to group discussion and consideration until you improved on it.

Perhaps that rather lengthy illustration allows us to look at the biblical narrative and our part in it in a new and significant way. Using the imagery we've evoked in the illustration, let's see how this might help us to read and engage with the Bible as a narrative in which both the Lord and we ourselves are intimately involved. I should underline at this point that this model does not lessen the significance of the Bible and its intrinsic authority in any way. Rather, it gives us another strategy for reading it and seeing our place in its story.

If the discovered play is a metaphor for the Bible and the world is the scene for the missing part to be enacted, what are the advantages of thinking about the Bible in this way? There are a good many that we could simply list at this point:

- This approach makes sure that we consider the story as *God's* story and not ours. Just as we would give full and proper reverence to the Bard if we were handling his play, so too with the Lord in considering the Bible. He is both author and central character. In his discussion of theodrama, Peter Phillips emphasises this conclusion: 'In the end, the Bible isn't about the history of the world, nor of Israel, nor of the church. Everything is discussed, the whole story told, from a theological perspective. What matters is God's activity, God's engagement, God's covenant love for his people and for his creation.'[54] If we were being true to the play, we'd want to be true to its author, its playwright – true to his intentions, true to the dynamic of the narrative, true to its characters and true to the envisioned finale. Just so with scripture, seen through the theodrama lens. We want to be true to the author's intentions, both explicit and implicit throughout the text. Not one of us is the leading character in the story; God is both author and leading role.

- This perspective indicates that reading scripture (that is, engaging with scripture) is not easy! It is, in fact, rather more complex than many of us realise. And because of that, we will need a community of people who love the text, who want to discuss its riches and its direction openly and with appropriate vulnerability, to come alongside us and to engage generously with God's word with us. That group may be the local church or a home group. This implies the need sometimes of 'experts' – in the shape of theologically trained and Spirit-gifted women and men or in the form of commentaries and books on the Bible.

- Theodrama allows for diverse opinions and perspectives on scripture. When a group gets together to read scripture like this, the aim is to learn from one another, to take on board other personal or cultural views, to allow an imaginative and improvised reading in order to generate discussion and progress.

- Theodrama encourages a less stark reading of the Bible. While doctrine is important, the notion of theodrama suggests to us that there are areas where we have to improvise our response because we don't have enough information or experience. Improvisation is common enough in the scriptural narrative itself. One or two examples will suffice at this point.

When the prostitute Rahab hid the spies, for example, we are told that she concealed them from the king of Jericho and told him that they had fled the city – which was a lie.[55] Many pages of Christian or Old Testament ethics have been written questioning whether Rahab chose a secondary or 'lesser' sin (lying) over a primary or 'greater' one (giving the men up to certain death). This question is magnified in that the Lord blessed her and her family with freedom from death when the city was later destroyed by Israel. But isn't it more likely that she simply improvised her response to the situation? On the basis of her limited knowledge of God – that the whole of Jericho feared him, that he'd fought on behalf of the Israelites, that he is 'God in heaven above and on the earth below' (Joshua 2:11) – she bargains with the spies for her life and that of her relatives. For that, she was saved and is included and honoured in the list of those who showed courageous and God-given faith (Hebrews 11:31). For a similar situation, look at Jeremiah 38:24–27, in which the prophet lies to escape his and the king's death.

The early church improvised in initially sharing everything they possessed to help the poor (Acts 2:44–45), demonstrating that the Lord's grace was working powerfully in their midst, so much so that there were no needy persons among them (Acts 4:33–34). Again, over the question of the circumcision of new Gentile believers and their keeping the law of Moses on entry to the church, the apostles and church leaders wrote to them that they were to 'abstain from food sacrificed to idols, from blood, from the meat of strangled animals and from sexual immorality' (Acts 15:29). This decision was based on the grace of God to the Gentiles and on Peter's comment that difficulties should not be placed in the way of Gentiles coming to faith in Jesus Christ (Acts 15:19).

Biblical improvisation isn't just making things up as you go along! In these two examples, we see Rahab and the early church improvising into a brand-new situation, but both are based on an understanding of who God is – the God of heaven and earth, the God of grace in Jesus Christ. Improvising comes from limited understanding and knowledge – just as it would if we found only a part of a Shakespearean play. We know as much as we have, but no more. We discern where the play is going but more in its direction than in the details of its conclusion. So too with scripture. From the Bible we glean an understanding of God and of his intentions for his people and the world in which we live. Theology comes before improvisation, indicative before imperative. However, when we try to read scripture on subjects such as marriage, divorce, nuclear war, housing problems, politics, mission, the church and its government, use of the internet, gay rights, animal testing and the like, we have some help, some instruction and history to work with, a divine trajectory, but perhaps not enough to be definitive about the detailed conclusions we reach. Knowing what we do, however, gives us enough to improvise, to move ahead and not simply to be inert for lack of clarity.

- Biblical improvisation gives us a way of reading the biblical text without always looking for 'right' and 'wrong', for black-and-white answers. Life and experience aren't that simple or straightforward. Biblical improvisation allows us to hold on to the things we see clearly, but to be courageous in the things that are not so certain. It encourages us sometimes to have a go without fear of failure,[56] to do our best though we know it isn't going to be 'good enough' or perfect, to join the narrative as best we can.

- Biblical improvisation reminds us that we need to think biblically. If we were looking at the play by Shakespeare, we'd need to think in a similar way to the playwright if we were going to finish the play and do him proud. It's not good enough to have completed the play but to have lost the plot! So too with the Bible. There is a danger of using proof texts and missing the point of God's word. To quote a text is not the same as thinking biblically – for that, we need to have grasped the whole narrative and to see ourselves in that divine story as best we can.

- It might be helpful to see one or two biblical passages as doing the same work as Shakespeare's prologue in *Romeo and Juliet*. Genesis 1 gives us more than a good clue about the whole story of the Bible: 'God saw all that he had made, and it was very good' (Genesis 1:31). John's opening prologue indicates the same narrative fleshed out in Jesus Christ (John 1:1–18). Can you think of any other passages that may play this role?

See for yourself

In your home group or with a number of friends, consider one of the following subjects, or a topic of your own choice, through the lens of theodrama: immigration, slavery, worship, working on Sundays, IVF treatment, discipleship. In each case we have some information, some biblical narrative that might help, but not a great deal. For each we might discern the conclusion in the direction of God's story and our inclusion in it. In what ways might we need to improvise our response? What would you consider to be suitable improvisation?

Part III

Micro-strategies: how to read the text

While macro-strategies encourage us to read the whole biblical narrative, micro-strategies suggest ways of reading that might help us to understand individual texts or passages of the Bible. Again, I would underline that these are not supposed to replace prayer and a disciplined waiting on the Lord. They are not a shortcut, but simply aids in reading scripture.

8

Ignatian Bible reading: the use of Christian imagination

In the Catholic Reformation of the 16th century the Society of Jesus (or Jesuits) was the most famous of the Catholic new orders. It was founded by Ignatius of Loyola (1491–1556) in 1534 and approved by Pope Paul III six years later. Originally a soldier, Ignatius was converted while convalescing from battle wounds sustained at Pamplona in 1521. In his meditation, he came to realise the mercy and grace of a fearful and awesome God. He translates the ideals of the Christian knight into the Christian priesthood through his book *The Spiritual Exercises*.[57] He describes what he intends by the phrase 'spiritual exercises':

> By the term Spiritual Exercises we mean every method of examination of conscience, meditation, contemplation, vocal or mental prayer, and other spiritual activities... For, just as taking a walk, traveling on foot, and running are physical exercises, so is the name of spiritual exercises given to any means of preparing and disposing our soul to rid itself of all its disordered affections and then, after their removal, of seeking and finding God's will in the ordering of our life for the salvation of our soul.[58]

We might notice from this that what Ignatius intends is not an intellectual exercise; it is meditating, contemplating, praying and so on. It is more about feeling than thinking, about openness to God and to oneself in his presence. It has to do with one's own salvation, fighting against sin and seeking the will of God. It's about loving Jesus more and becoming a more faithful and committed follower.

The book, which has become a classic of Christian spirituality, is divided into four weeks.

The first week calls its readers to reflect on God's boundless love and to lament their sins. Significantly, sin is defined in relational not legal terms: we sin when we turn our back on God himself. The first week ends with a meditation on Christ's call to follow him.

The second week teaches us what it is to follow Jesus Christ, to be his disciples. There are meditations on Christ's birth and baptism, his ministry, the sermon on the mount and his raising Lazarus from the dead.

The third week encourages us to meditate on the last supper, Christ's Passion and his death.

The fourth week looks at Christ's resurrection and his post-resurrection appearances to the disciples. Ignatius asks us to consider ways in which we can serve Jesus better and show the love of God in the contemporary world.

In contemplation, Ignatius encourages us to use sanctified imagin-ation and to place ourselves into the scriptural stories of Jesus – stories of his activity rather than his teaching. In the second week, for example, Ignatius contemplates the nativity of Jesus. He starts with prayer. He imagines Mary and Joseph with a maid. They are going to Bethlehem, Mary on a donkey. Then he contemplates the place – in this case the road from Nazareth to Bethlehem: its length and breadth, whether it is level or rough and uneven, whether it traverses hills or valleys and so on. Upon arrival, they enter 'the cave of the nativity'. How large is it? How high or low? How will it be prepared?

Now, he says, look at the people involved: Mary, Joseph and, after his birth, the baby Jesus. Ignatius sees himself as a servant (or slave) present at the scene, looking at them and respectfully serving them. The next thing to do is to mark what is being said and by whom. Contemplation turns to seeking to draw some spiritual profit from the scene, seeing that all this was done for *me*, for *my* salvation – the poverty, the hunger and thirst, the heat and cold, the injuries and offence, that Jesus may die on the cross.

From this example from *The Spiritual Exercises* you can see that the method of entering into the text of scripture encourages us to be open to what we find there, to be attentive to details (taste, sight, smell, sound and feeling, and what is going on in the event), to encounter Jesus in his journey for us and ultimately to know Jesus more intimately, present with us.

Let's detail this approach to reading biblical passages:

- Find a quiet and peaceful place to do this exercise.

- Pray that the Lord would quieten you and give you peace. Relax in his presence. As much as you can, be determined to encounter the Lord through this exercise. Be ready to engage with God's word, not simply to read it.

- Find a passage from the gospels in which Jesus interacts with other people – it may be a crowd or a group of Pharisees, an individual or his disciples.

- Read the passage two or three times, slowly and carefully, taking in the whole story together with the details. Allow the story to become familiar to you. Is there something that stands out for you?

- Close your eyes, if that helps, and try to picture the scene. Through your imagination, place yourself there with Jesus on that day.

  - Where does the scene take place?
  - Who is there in the scene?
  - What is Jesus doing?
  - What is he saying?
  - What are the sights, sounds, smells?
  - What can you touch or feel?
  - Which character are you – part of the crowd, a disciple, someone waiting to be healed?
  - How are people reacting to Jesus?
  - How do you feel about what's happening? You may be feeling any number of emotions: perhaps joy, sorrow, peace, puzzlement, love, disappointment.

- Participate as fully as possible in the scene; interact with the other characters and with Jesus himself.

- Finally, speak directly to the Lord in prayer, telling him frankly how the exercise made you feel, seeking to get close to him by his Spirit.

- Reread the biblical passage. Has engagement with it added to your spiritual understanding?

It's a good idea to review each reading of scripture. It's worth remembering that this isn't an exercise in imagination per se but an exercise in biblical engagement, an attempt to read the text more thoroughly, seeking a closer bond with Jesus Christ through it.

See for yourself

Follow the steps outlined above as you read the following passages from the gospels:

- Jesus anointed by a sinful woman (Luke 7:36–50)
- Jesus feeding the 5,000 (Luke 9:10–17)
- Jesus and Zacchaeus, the tax collector (Luke 19:1–10)

Remember, this isn't a test of your imagination; it's an exercise in Bible reading and engagement. By the end of it, you should feel that you've really understood the text and that you've somehow come closer to Jesus himself. As with all our reading of scripture, it should end in praise and gratitude for who he has shown himself to be.

9

Praying the Bible: a garland of four strands

Early in 1535 the German reformer Martin Luther wrote an open letter, 'How One Should Pray, for Master Peter the Barber', or 'A Simple Way to Pray'. Peter Beskendorf was Luther's hairdresser and had apparently been talking to the reformer about the difficulty of prayer. The reformer's response was to write this short book. It is principally about prayer, but, as you'll see, it gives us a significant way of reading scripture, too.

A garland of four strands

Luther explains that if he has time he takes each commandment, for example, one after another, and divides each commandment into four parts, 'thereby fashioning a garland of four strands'. He then consciously considers each as different aspects of his reading:

- First, instruction ('which is what it is intended to be,' he says). At this point, the question he asks himself is simply what the Lord demands of him 'so earnestly'.
- Then, he turns his consideration of the commandment to thanksgiving.
- Then to confession.
- And, lastly, to prayer or supplication.

Later, Luther speaks of this as a commandment's 'fourfold aspect', implying the strength of the aspects together, like a rope made from four separate cords intertwined for greater strength. These help to shape Luther's contemplation of the text.

Let's look at how this is accomplished as Luther reads the first commandment.[59] He starts by reading or reciting the first commandment, 'You shall have no other gods before me' (Exodus 20:3), to himself, out loud. The four strands of instruction, thanksgiving, confession and supplication follow, but what we need to notice is the thought or meditation that has gone on between reciting the commandment and the strands. His repeated reading of the commandment encourages him to think through the implications in each strand. This is clear from what he prays.

- First, under 'instruction', Luther suggests that in this commandment God, declaring himself to be *his* God, expects Luther to trust him alone in everything – actually, for Luther, that is part and parcel of what it is to be a Christian.

- Second, under 'thanksgiving', the reformer is grateful to God, who 'unasked, unbidden and unmerited' has offered to be *his* God. We have sought after all sorts of other things to trust in, he admits, but the Lord, in remarkable and unmerited grace, has told us that he intends to be our God. 'How could we ever in all eternity thank him enough!' Luther rejoices.

- Third, he confesses to having provoked God by his idolatries: 'I repent of these and ask for his grace.'

- Last, he prays that God would give him understanding of the commandments and the ability to confidently live by them. In this way we see that prayer allows God the initiative in our lives.

Luther shapes his response to each commandment in the same way: following the pattern of instruction, thanksgiving, confession and prayer.

What Luther offers is a form of *lectio divina* or 'godly reading'. But what is this? In short, *lectio divina* refers to a prayerful reading of a scripture passage with openness to and expectancy of God speaking through it. As you can see, the definition itself singles out three important elements of this exercise: reading scripture, praying and being open to the work of the Holy Spirit both through the reading and in response to the prayer.

So with this reading strategy we meditate on the passage with the following four aspects or 'strands' uppermost in our minds, seeking the Lord's help:

- instruction, or teaching
- thanksgiving, or grateful praise
- confession, or repentance
- prayer, or supplication

It's important that we see this short list as applying directly to ourselves. We can help ensure this by turning the various strands or aspects into pointed questions – something like the following:

- Instruction, or teaching: what is the Lord seeking to teach me from this passage? What do I need to know?
- Thanksgiving, or grateful praise: what should I be grateful for on reading this portion of scripture?
- Confession, or repentance: how does this passage impinge on my conscience, and what in it encourages me to confess particular sins? What sins shall I confess?
- Prayer, or supplication: what do I now need to pray for, to cry out to God for?

This focus on us is not intended to centre all things on ourselves in an egocentric way, as if we are the most important element in this spiritual exchange. Rather, a focus on ourselves here helps to ensure the intimate and relational link that Luther wishes to build between the reader, the word of God and God himself. In fact, more than that: it is important for us to realise God beyond the Bible, to relate in a personal way to the God whom we experience and who confronts us through the word.

The stages in this reading are as follows:

Pray for God to help. It's important that we rely on the Holy Spirit in this exercise.

Read the passage. Do this thoughtfully, slowly and prayerfully two or three times.

Think out loud. Brainstorm aloud about the content of the biblical passage: what are the main themes; who are the main characters; are there any comparisons being made; what is it telling me to believe and do?

Keep God and Jesus as central, not self. As we've seen above, the overriding teaching of scripture is of the wonderful salvation granted to fallen human beings by the grace of God through Jesus Christ. The Lord is central to that narrative: not Israel, not the church, not us, but God. It helps tremendously if we keep that in mind as we read scripture. This works itself out if generally we look first at what can be learned of God, then about ourselves.

Consider the four strands. Do this personally and honestly.

Conclude with prayer. This should be related to your thinking so far.

Wait on the Lord. Anticipate that he'll speak to you through scripture and meditation.[60]

See for yourself

Here is a short list of passages that you might use to practise this strategy in biblical engagement. Take one at a time and apply what you've learned from Luther's method.

- Genesis 28:10–17
- Psalm 113
- Habakkuk 3:17–19
- Luke 9:28–36
- 1 Peter 2:9–10

10

Being precedes acting: indicative and imperative

It's sometimes helpful to be able to see a pattern or structure to passages in the Bible. This present strategy does just that; it highlights how many of the instructions in the Bible – imperatives – are grounded in certain truths about God – indicatives.[61] Before examining the relationship between them, let me explain these two important words.

An indicative is a statement of fact; it says how things are. In simple terms, they are 'is' statements. A straightforward example might be 'I am a Christian'. That phrase is a statement of fact; it says what is the case, who I am. It is indicative.

An imperative, on the other hand, is a command or instruction. It says that something ought to be done; they are 'ought' statements. An example is 'Be holy'. It commands action, a lifestyle; it expects a response. It is imperative.

Biblical indicatives tend to express the fact that the new life in Christ is a work of God; its origin is in the death and resurrection of the Lord and comes into being through the work of the Holy Spirit. We, as believers, are a new creation, a member of Christ, a temple of the Holy Spirit. These are all salvific indicatives, statements of fact about us because we've been saved by the gracious activity of God. There are many more, of course. Can you think of others?

The question for our purposes is whether there is a relationship or a structure that exists between the indicative and the imperative. Can we see this when we read the Bible?

As we shall see in the examples that follow, a pattern or structure is apparent. Here it is in simple form:

indicative → therefore → imperative
'is' → therefore → 'ought'

In other words, the New Testament imperatives are not just generic moral teachings; they are based on the fact of a new nature, given by God through the Holy Spirit. They are a call to obedience to the one who has created that relationship with us. The new life given in Christ is to be continually worked out by the Christian believer. So we see that godly behaviour is the consequence, not the cause, of the newness of the believer's new being.

With that introduction, let's look at some examples from the apostle Paul before turning to other parts of scripture.

Romans 12:1–2

Imagine that you're reading through Paul's letter to the Romans. You reach Romans 12:1, 'Therefore, I urge you, brothers and sisters, in view of God's mercy, to offer your bodies as a living sacrifice, holy and pleasing to God – this is your true worship.' Here the apostle is exhorting believers in Rome to live in a certain way. He wants them to give themselves in holiness sacrificially to God in a way that will be pleasing to him – that is, to God. He summarises that sacrificial obedience in the words of verse 2: negatively, they must 'not conform to the pattern of this world'; positively, they are to 'be transformed by the renewing of' their minds.' (The word translated 'minds' is *nous*, which indicates moral thinking in particular.) So the apostle is asking for action, for change, for transformation in their thinking and behaviour – that is the imperative of Paul's message. This is what they ought to do, the way they ought to live. What is he grounding that change in? What is the indicative, the 'is' statement upon which the imperative rests? Paul tells us that it's 'in view of God's mercy' (v. 1). That is, because of the mercy of God, they are to behave in a certain way.

Remember that the pattern is 'indicative' therefore 'imperative'; the 'is' statement therefore the 'ought' exhortation. Here in the opening verses of Romans 12, Paul actually gives us the word 'therefore'! The pattern in this passage is:

The mercy of God towards them → **therefore** → **not conforming to the world's pattern**

The mercy of God towards them → **therefore** → **transforming their thinking**

Because the Lord has been merciful towards us, says Paul, we ought to live in a godly, countercultural way. The interesting thing in this context is that the apostle has been at pains to show them the mercy of God throughout the letter. Salvation is merciful, and Paul has used ideas closely aligned to that: kindness (2:4), patience (9:22; 11:22), love (5:5; 8:35, 39), grace (1:7, 3:24 and so on).[62] It is clear in the way he outlines the divine faithfulness to Jew and Gentile alike (chapters 1—3), justification by faith and life in Christ (chapters 4—7) and life by the Spirit (chapter 8). However, it's interesting that mercy is a recurrent keynote theme of chapters 9—11.[63] So the apostle Paul uses the language of sacrifice to urge Christian believers to give themselves to God, the God who has shown such amazing mercy towards them in Jesus Christ. It's a clear example of the imperative of godly living being directly related to the indicative statement of the gospel: God has been merciful, *therefore* live sacrificially.

Before we draw any conclusions from this to help us to engage with the Bible more significantly, let's notice a few more examples.

Philippians 2:12–13

Here, following the well-known passage about the humility and exaltation of Jesus (Philippians 2:5–11), the apostle urges his readers to 'continue to work out [their] salvation with fear and trembling' (v. 12), adding that it is 'God who works in [them] to will and to act in order to fulfil his good purpose' (v. 13). Here, Paul is not telling the Philippians to accomplish their salvation – that's already been given; it's theirs as a gift of God (the indicative, the 'is' statement). But Paul *is* encouraging them to finish, to carry to conclusion, to apply that salvation with faith and perseverance to the end (the imperative, the 'ought' statement). Fascinatingly, he also indicates that there is something of the role of God in the obedience expected from them ('for it is God who works in you', v. 13). The indicative is a divine gift, but so is the imperative, says Paul. Divine grace gives salvation in Christ; it also motivates and energises the believer in their Christian walk through the work of the Holy Spirit. Here, then, the pattern is the same as we've observed before:

You have salvation as a gift → therefore → work out your salvation in practice

1 Corinthians 6:12–20

The context of these verses is complex and seems strange to 21st-century people. However, the passage shows the same pattern again and will further clarify what I'm seeking to show. Suffice it to say, at this point, that the Corinthian believers seemed to undervalue or even to devalue the physical aspect of life and, consistently with this, they used the maxim 'I have the right to do anything' (v. 12) – even to the point of having sex with prostitutes. What they did in the body didn't matter, they said; only the spirit counted for anything. They had presumed that the body (as physical) had no permanent value because of its deterioration at death (see v. 14). So it seems that nothing done in the body had moral value for them.

For our purposes we need to see how the apostle counters their argument. He does so by using the now-familiar pattern:

indicative → therefore → imperative

Read the passage slowly and see if you can discern this pattern or structure in Paul's counterargument. What does he exhort them to do? What does he base this exhortation upon?

Whether we understand the prostitute as one involved in temple worship doesn't really matter for our purposes. The imperatives that the apostle uses are straightforward enough. First, he puts the exhortation (imperative) negatively: they are to flee, to shun, that is, to take strong evasive action, in this area. They are to flee sexual immorality (v. 18). The second imperative he employs is positive: 'Therefore honour God with your bodies' (v. 20).

As we've come to expect, these imperatives rest upon or are grounded in significant organising indicatives -- three, in fact. First, Paul says, 'Do you not know that your bodies are members of Christ himself?' (v. 15). The second significant indicative is found in verse 19: 'Do you not know that your bodies are temples of the Holy Spirit, who is in you, whom you have received from God?' It's interesting that the question form is identical and that both questions imply that in fact they *did* know, or certainly should have known. The third indicative comes in verses 19–20 and is followed by the 'therefore' of the final imperative: 'You are not your own; you were bought at a price. *Therefore* honour God with your bodies' (italics added).

What seems to be happening here is that the apostle searches for statements of truth concerning the status and condition of the believer that will answer the question 'Why should/shouldn't I behave in such and such a way?' Having discovered three such reasons (indicatives), he brings them to bear on the pastoral situation in the Corinthian church.

Paul isn't the only New Testament writer to work on this indicative/ imperative pattern, but he is possibly the most clearly devoted to its use. Here are some other examples from the Old and New Testaments:

Consecrate yourselves and be holy (*imperative 1*), because I am the Lord your God (*indicative 1*). Keep my decrees and follow them (*imperative 2*). I am the Lord, who makes you holy (*indicative 2*).
LEVITICUS 20:7–8

Therefore, since we are receiving a kingdom that cannot be shaken (*indicative 1*), let us be thankful (*imperative 1*), and so worship God acceptably with reverence and awe (*imperative 2*), for our 'God is a consuming fire' (*indicative 2*).
HEBREWS 12:28–29

You too, be patient (*imperative 1*) and stand firm (*imperative 2*), because the Lord's coming is near (*indicative*).
JAMES 5:8

The end of all things is near (*indicative*). Therefore be alert (*imperative 1*) and of a sober mind (*imperative 2*) so that you may pray.
1 PETER 4:7

As a last example, read Psalm 117 – the shortest psalm in scripture. Its exhortations are based on the pattern we're looking at.

Praise the Lord, all you nations;
    extol him, all you peoples
For great is his love towards us,
    and the faithfulness of the Lord endures forever.

Praise the Lord.

Where are the imperatives in this short psalm? What indicatives do they rest on? It sometimes helps to turn things around a bit and to get the word 'therefore' into view. Look at the following turnaround of Psalm 117.

God's love toward us is great (*indicative 1*)
　His faithfulness endures forever (*indicative 2*)
Therefore
Praise the Lord, all you nations (*imperative 1*)
　Extol him, all you peoples (*imperative 2*)

Praise the Lord (*imperative 1 repeated to conclude the psalm*)

There are obvious advantages to engaging with scripture with this indicative/imperative pattern in mind.

- Because the indicative statements of our faith nearly always reflect the divine salvific activity of God upon and in us, reading like this centres our thinking on God, first and foremost. It reminds us that we live as we do because we have been changed by the Holy Spirit, that we are being transformed into Christ's image and that our lives, therefore, ought to reflect the fact that we are a new creation in Christ. Being does precede acting; a renewed nature comes before holiness.

- The imperatives are grounded in the reality that has been given through Christ; they appeal to it, as we've seen, and they intend to bring it to full development (Philippians 2:12–13). So reading the Bible with this in mind encourages us to realise not only why we find godliness so difficult, but also that we are not alone in trying to live out the gospel – graciously, the Holy Spirit is part and parcel of both the indicative and the imperative. On the one hand, he gives us new life in Christ and makes us a new creation, and on the other hand he motivates us and energises us for Christian living. Reading like this gives us confidence and helps us to know that our 'labour in the Lord is not in vain' (1 Corinthians 15:58).

- Reading with this indicative/imperative structure in mind reminds us that what we believe is vitally important to how we live. In other words, it will encourage us to look for biblical truth about God, the world, the church and so on, as well as hints and indications on how we should therefore live. If one is based on the other, if one is the foundation of the other, then it makes considerable sense to say that both are important for us.

See for yourself

Look at the following biblical passages and find the indicatives and imperatives in them. Then attempt to see how they relate to each other: how are the imperatives grounded in the indicatives, the instructions in the theology? What is the force of the relationship between them? How do they suggest the centrality of God and the believer's responsibility?

- Deuteronomy 26:16–19
- Leviticus 20:26
- Romans 6:1–14
- Colossians 3:1–14

11

Engaging Bible stories: a narrative retelling

When we read biblical narratives, we sometimes find one of two things: either that they are just too complicated or that we read without genuine and worthwhile engagement. The frustration of the former is that at the conclusion of the story we still have no real understanding of what has been recounted. The difficulty of the latter is that, though we have understood the story, it has meant nothing to us personally, in terms of either our comprehension and awareness or godly application of anything we've read.

As a boy, I could never work out what adults meant by the saying 'More haste, less speed'. I think it was the close juxtaposition of the synonyms 'haste' and 'speed' that fooled me. However, in our spiritual lives generally and our reading of scripture specifically, the saying has a lot to offer. As I've implied earlier in this book, biblical engagement implies a deliberate, thoughtful, slower, incremental progression and development through the text, not simply reading. And this purposeful engaging applies equally to reading narratives as it does to the more explicitly theological texts of scripture, such as the apostle Paul's letters. It pays to move through the text slowly; it will be faster in the long run.

One way we can move constructively slowly through the text is by retelling the narrative. This exercise will help us to concentrate our thinking on the text itself within its broader context. Here, however, let me repeat something I've said already – always pray for the Lord's Spirit to aid you before you start reading. Ask him to open your mind to what he wants to say to you through the text, to give you wisdom and faith. Retelling the narrative isn't a shortcut to biblical understanding or to seeking the Spirit's aid!

Let's start with a well-known and fairly lengthy story: the flood narrative of Genesis 6:5—9:17. Let's imagine, too, that you've read the earlier chapters of Genesis, and now you've reached this narrative in your consecutive reading. Better still, why not read the book of Genesis to this point before proceeding?

The reading

Read the flood narrative slowly, once or twice. Then, begin to retell the story by taking blocks of text (or narrative) at a time. Remember that this isn't an exercise in storytelling; no one else is going to hear this – unless you want them to. This is a retelling of the story for your own benefit, in order to engage with the narrative more carefully than if you were simply reading it.

The following is my attempt. Yours will be different, reflecting who you are and your own interests, faith and theology. I offer my attempt as an example only. As I recount the story it's likely to remind me of other things, such as other biblical narratives, and to make me emphasise characters, narrative shape or theology as I go through, because I'm doing this slowly and thoughtfully with an eye to understanding, not simply moving on to the next episode. I think you'll see what I mean.

The story

The Lord looked upon men and women and saw how violently wicked they were – even their thoughts were continually evil in his holy sight. As he looked, he deeply regreted making people to populate the earth and decided to destroy every one of them – except Noah, whom he realised was holy, a good man, a man he loved.

The Lord explained this to Noah before telling him to build an ark, giving him very specific instructions. He explained that he was going to flood the earth, but that he was entering into a covenant with Noah and through him with his wife, his sons (Shem, Ham and Japheth) and their wives, too. Noah was commanded to bring in two of every kind of animal and food as well. Noah, because he feared God, did exactly what he was told.

Seven days before the flood waters appeared, Noah and his family, the animals and the birds – clean and unclean – entered the ark just as God had commanded. The Lord shut the door on them, and they were safe. It rained for 40 days, and the waters rose so high that they covered even the tallest mountains on the earth. Obviously, every living thing outside of the ark that God had protected died. All those inside were miraculously saved by God's grace.

Eventually God remembered Noah and his family and made the waters recede. Sending out a dove to see if there was dry land proved futile at first, as the dove returned to the ark. Noah sent it out again, but it returned, then again, at which point it departed the ark for good. The earth was dry again!

Sometime later, God told Noah and his family and the animals to come out from the ark. Noah, being righteous and grateful, immediately built an altar, sacrificed some of the animals and birds and then worshipped the Lord. This sacrifice the Lord smelled, promising never to destroy the earth nor humanity in the same way again. However, on reflection, the Lord recognised that men and women would remain evil and wicked, even after the flood – both its destruction and its continuing threat. In words which remind us of the creation story ('Be fruitful and multiply', etc.) God renewed his covenant with Noah, and through him with humanity, putting a rainbow as a clear covenant sign for people of all future generations to see and trust.

The reflection

What I've attempted to do in retelling the story is not to get down all the details but rather to explore the narrative shape, the characters and the salient facts. So the story I've told is necessarily less exacting than the biblical one. It does help me, though, to reflect. Things that I may have missed in simply reading Genesis 6—9 through are more obvious to me.

For example, in telling the story I realised that it begins and ends with the same words: God says to himself and then later 'in his heart' that men and women are and will remain evil ('every inclination of the [thoughts of the] human heart is evil from childhood' – Genesis 6:5; 8:21). The repetition is staggering in its intent. The first utterance of the phrase summons the destruction of humanity *because* of their wickedness; the second suggests that the Lord will be patient and gracious to humanity *despite* the fact of their wickedness. So, remarkably, the writer seems to be saying that the flood period affected God as well as humanity. Noah is made truly grateful for divine protection (hence the worship); God recognises the vulnerability and pain involved in being patient with a sinful humanity, and what it will cost him to have a continuing relationship with us.

Retelling the story also made me realise again the significance of God's role in this and Noah's response to it. It is the Lord who loves Noah over against the rest of the earth's population, establishing a covenant with him. It is God who tells him to build an ark, who saves Noah and his family, who shuts the ark's door in protection, who remembers Noah, who commands the ark's inhabitants to come out into dryness and safety, who smells the sacrifice and accepts it, who turns away from his intention to destroy the earth and who promises not to flood it again. The story is about God, all about God. The Lord instigates; Noah responds. Noah is certainly righteous – he is obedient, faithful and grateful, a great example of faith (see Hebrews 11:7) – but significantly the Old Testament narrative underlines divine gracious action more than it does Noah's righteousness.

The details (the ark's dimensions, the number of flood days and so on), which perhaps serve to make the story credible, I've largely left out of my recounting. If anything, the ark's measurements, the exact numbers of animals and living creatures, the days counted so carefully and so on show me precision and, importantly, order. These emphasise divine creativity, orderliness in the face of chaos and sovereign control – themes that will surface again and again in the overall biblical narrative (starting with the creation itself).

The story again

At this point, it's good to reread the Genesis account, not to make sure you have everything in your retelling but to allow the Holy Spirit to build on the emphases of what you've discovered. To engage with scripture is to wait upon God to show you from his word what he wants you to know. Pray that he might do so as you reread this portion.

See for yourself

To practise this strategy, you could use the following biblical narratives or any others you would like to engage with. *Read the story* once or twice, slowly and thoughtfully. *Retell the story*, attempting to pick out salient details and trying to emphasise what the Bible emphasises – plot, characters, narrative shape and so on. *Reflect on your retelling* and read the narrative again with a prayerful attitude, mindful of what the Lord wants to teach you.

- Judges 16: Samson, Delilah and his death
- 2 Chronicles 1: Solomon and his prayer for wisdom
- Mark 6:45–56: Jesus walks on water
- Luke 8:22–39: two of Jesus' miracles
- Acts 3:1–10: Peter heals a lame beggar
- Acts 10: Peter and Cornelius meet

12

Narratives are about people: sorting through the characters

Stories, generally, are about people, and biblical stories are no exception; they are about people too. So it's important that we look at biblical narratives sometimes by giving due emphasis to the characters involved. In this way, we can clearly differentiate characters in a narrative – a discernment that might help us to see what's happening and how to helpfully read the passage.

Take the narrative of Exodus 12:31–51. Imagine that you've been reading through the book of Exodus and you come upon this portion about the exodus of the Israelites from Egypt. (It would be helpful to read this passage at this point, before going further.) Who are the characters involved here? A careful reading might discern the Egyptians and their leader, Pharaoh; the Israelites and their leaders, Moses and Aaron; and the Lord himself. Already, you might see that a significant interpretation is developing simply by suggesting the parallel patterns. Let's look at each one in more detail.

Pharaoh seeks to retain a residue of control (despite the plagues and suffering experienced), as he tells Moses and Aaron to leave with the people of Israel, to leave his people alone (vv. 31–32). There is urgency about it – noticeably, his command occurs in the middle of the night. Strikingly, the Egyptian citizens have a similar urgency, requesting the Israelites to leave them in fear of their own death, giving them articles of silver and gold and clothing (v. 33).

The second character is the Israelites. When the narrative speaks of the Israelites, it makes every effort to indicate a definable group, a community of people. It numbers them (600,000 men, plus women and children; v. 37); they obey Moses' instructions (v. 35); they move out of Egypt in 'divisions' (vv. 41, 51). These are the people who have obeyed God and kept the Passover, who have awaited their chance to depart the land of slavery. This sense of community is strengthened by the regulations that follow concerning the Passover meal, which is to be celebrated each year on this specific date (v. 42): no foreigner is to eat it, unless they have their whole household circumcised (vv. 43, 48); slaves are to be circumcised before partaking of it (v. 44); and no one outside the community may eat the Passover (vv. 45, 49). In short, 'The whole community of Israel must celebrate it' (v. 47). It's both the restricted partaking of the Passover and the eating of it together that help define Israel as a community here.

The third character in the narrative is the Lord. He is the most significant, of course. As we read the story we see clearly that he holds the narrative, that is, the actual events, together: the people are leaving Egypt to worship the Lord (v. 31); the Lord had made the Egyptians 'favourably disposed' to the Israelites (v. 36); he 'kept vigil that night to bring them out of Egypt' (v. 42); and we're told that 'on that very day the Lord brought the Israelites out of Egypt' (v. 51).

So as we explore this paradigmatic episode in the life of Israel, as we engage fully with the narrative, looking carefully at the characters involved, our reading underlines the message of the passage. It seems to underscore God's sovereignty over the events and, perhaps more importantly, his election of and his love and grace towards the people of Israel. There are two parties opposing one another, Egypt and Israel, but the story indicates clearly that Israel wins the tussle because the Lord manifests his grace towards them and redeems them from a slavery that has lasted 430 years (v. 41).

This would naturally lead to reflecting upon the Lord's goodness to his people, on the idea and experience of election (or calling), on divine protection and keeping, and on the meaning of community and tradition. Employing what we've gained from both the linear and the triangular models (see part II) we might explore these themes into the New Testament and beyond.

Having delineated the three 'characters' in the narrative, it's a good practice to reread the biblical passage. Do so prayerfully, allowing the Holy Spirit to teach you what the passage says about the Lord himself, about his people and about the biblical story that by grace you have joined and become part of.

See for yourself

Take each of the following passages and see how discerning the characters involved can help you engage with the biblical narrative. *Read the passage* once or twice slowly, with prayer. Try to *differentiate the characters* involved, asking yourself why they are as they are in the story. How does this help understand the narrative? *Reread the story and pray* for the Lord's application to you specifically.

- Genesis 12:1–9: the call of Abram
- Deuteronomy 34: the death of Moses
- 2 Chronicles 36:15–23: the fall of Jerusalem
- Matthew 14:22–36: Jesus walks on water
- Luke 13:10–17: Jesus heals a crippled woman on the sabbath
- Acts 19:1–22: the apostle Paul in Ephesus

13

Working out the topic sentence: everything else hangs on it

Some biblical passages will have a clear topic sentence. A topic sentence is one that expresses the main idea of the paragraph in which it occurs; it tells the reader what the paragraph is about; it determines the paragraph's content. Everything else seems to hang from it, to qualify it, to enlarge upon it. It makes sense that if we're able to discern the topic sentence of a passage, its shape and its meaning should become much clearer.

The apostle Paul's argument in Galatians 5:1–13 is probably the clearest example of this in the New Testament. Paul writes, 'It is for freedom that Christ has set us free' (v. 1), and all that he argues below that sentence hangs from it, explaining it, elucidating its implications. I've explored this passage at some length in my book about prayer, *Praying the Bible with Luther*,[64] so let's look elsewhere for examples and see how this strategy works.

Genesis 1:1—2:3

The Bible actually begins with a topic sentence: 'In the beginning God created the heavens and the earth' (Genesis 1:1). This topic sentence seems to tell us what the chapter is about. We need to take the topic sentence particularly seriously, for the rest of this amazing passage hangs from that statement: it describes what is meant by it, and it elaborates the truth of it.

'In the beginning God created the heavens and the earth.' At the very beginning of everything except God, the beginning of time, of physicality itself, God created. The writer informs us that his God, the God of Israel, is the one and only creator of everything there is ('the heavens and the earth' is an all-inclusive phrase). There is no other God like him. He is the imaginative, immensely powerful, outgoing (in its literal sense), wise God, who created both the heavens (the immeasurable sky, the uncountable stars, the planets) and the earth (the corporeality of who we are and what we have around us in all its diversity and beauty, its calm and its force). He alone did this; he and no one else. God is God; we know this because of what he's made and continues to sustain: he 'created the heavens and the earth'.

This topic sentence is a statement about the uniqueness of God and the powerful creativity of God. Interestingly, and notably, the passage very nearly concludes with this comment: 'Thus the heavens and the earth were completed in all their vast array' (Genesis 2:1). This stresses that we were right to point to the opening sentence as the topic sentence (the determinative sentence) of the passage, for it finishes the narrative where it began, at God's creation of everything we see.

The rest of Genesis 1 elaborates on this statement. It's a good strategy to ask questions of a topic sentence. Here we might ask: how did God create everything? Where did he create everything? What is included in that creation? Why did he create? You'll see at once that all the questions we're interested in won't necessarily be answered from Genesis 1. Indeed, some, like the reason for creation, may never be answered in any satisfactory way. But asking them expands our thinking at this point and makes us more alert.

Immediately following the topic sentence, 'In the beginning God created the heavens and the earth', the writer says that 'the earth was formless and empty' and covered with darkness (v. 2). Given what follows, this is significant, for what follows is order, life, fullness and light. Here, then, in verse 2, is a picture of chaos before the breath (the wind or spirit) of God creates. What are the relevant points to note about the divine creation? If in the beginning God created the heavens and the earth, then what was it like?

- Divine creation is spoken. Time and again the writer of Genesis 1 states that God speaks and things are created. Things come into being through his effortless command. 'God said, "Let there be light," and there was light' (v. 3) – it's as simple and yet as mystifyingly profound as that. God said let there be sky (v. 6), land, producing vegetation, and sea (v.v. 9–12), lights in the sky (v. 14), living creatures to inhabit the waters (v. 20), living creatures on the land (v. 24) and human beings (v. 26), and they were created. God said, God said, God said, and (simply) the repeated refrain, 'it was so'. God's powerful word creates, 'and it was so'.

- Divine creation is ordered. Repetition gives the chapter its shape and structure. The careful ordering of the narrative emphasises the order of creation. The numbering of the days of creative activity is the main backbone of the chapter: 'And there was evening, and there was morning' – the first day (v. 5), the second day (v. 8), the third day (v. 13), the fourth day (v. 19), the fifth day (v. 23), the sixth day (v. 31), and 'By the seventh day God had finished the work he had been doing' (2:2). The repetition of the phrase 'And God said' eight times throughout the chapter adds to this effect, as does the repeated comment, after verse 9, 'God saw that it was good.' The writer considers the work of God as ordered, over against the chaos of existence, perhaps, and stresses that here. God is a God of order, of stability, reliable in all he does.

- Divine creation is named. The fact that the Lord names almost everything in his creation seems significant. It is there in the narrative: God calls things by their name: 'day' and 'night' (v. 5), 'sky' (v. 8), 'land' and 'sea' (v. 10). This is important because, on reading this, I am also thinking of Adam naming Eve, of the Lord renaming so many Old Testament people, of Jesus renaming disciples like Peter, of God knowing our names. Names are significant in scripture; they define people and things. As God creates, he names.

- Divine creation is plentiful. Verses 11 and 12 emphasise the vegetation, again through simple repetition – 'seed-bearing plants' (v. 11), 'plants bearing seed' (v. 12) – giving a sense of life, reproduction and abundance. Similarly, the water 'teems' with life (v. 21), and the Lord commands the fish to 'increase in number and fill the water in the seas' (v. 22). Adam and Eve are told to 'be fruitful and… fill the earth' (v. 28).

- Divine creation climaxes in the creation of humanity. It is interesting that only at the creation of man and woman does the Lord deliberate within himself, 'Let us make human beings' (v. 26), making them in his image or likeness, somehow reflecting him in the world he has made for them. This is underlined, 'So God created human beings in his own image, in the image of God he created them; male and female he created them' (v. 27), at which point the Lord gives them everything – a wonderful display of generous grace.

- Divine creation is good. From the third day of creating, the Lord looks upon what he's made and, the writer tells us, 'the Lord saw that it was good'. This is repeated five times (vv. 9, 11, 18, 21, 25) before it reaches its climax and final form at the close of day six: 'God saw all that he had made, and it was very good' (v. 31).

- Divine creation concludes with rest. Only after the creation is complete does it say that the Lord rested. However, it is noteworthy that he made the seventh day of creation 'holy' by resting upon it (2:3).

We've certainly not exhausted what we might discover from Genesis 1, but what we have done demonstrates how the topic sentence ('In the beginning God created the heavens and the earth') determines the rest of the chapter, elaborating on the theme, focusing our attention on the two elements, 'God' and 'the heavens and the earth', and their relationship. It's clearly not intrinsically a scientific account, nor is it a historical one – it doesn't need to be. Genesis 1 is what we call myth; that is, a narrative that tells us something significant, in this case, about humanity as the pinnacle of divine creating activity and about God as sovereign and generous creator of everything and the divine giver of all things to humanity.

Engaging the passage by looking first at the topic sentence has led us to see the whole of the chapter as hanging upon that foundational idea. Exploring the remainder helps us to focus on some of the intricacies of what the passage is about. It helps us, too, to reflect on who God is and on our relationship with him as creator and benefactor in Jesus Christ. It reminds us that right from the beginning God loved his creation and humanity in particular: 'it was good'; indeed, 'it was very good'![65]

Genesis 22:1–19

If we look at the very difficult passage of Abraham going to sacrifice his son Isaac in Genesis 22, we can see that discovering the topic sentence becomes a very useful way of engaging with the story. Again, the topic sentence is at the beginning of the chapter: 'Some time later God tested Abraham' (v. 1). That's it! You'll see again that the whole narrative hangs on this statement: God tested Abraham. Verse 2 gives us the horrifying content of the test, 'Take your son, your only son, whom you love… sacrifice him.' We cannot imagine anything worse, but there it is in all its biblical starkness.

Verses 3–10 graphically demonstrate the patriarch's faith and confidence in God as he responds to the Lord's testing, right up to the point at which he raises his knife 'to slay his son' (v. 10). The verses that follow (vv. 11–14) give the resolution of the test – finding the ram to sacrifice instead of the son and Abraham's declaration of faith, 'The Lord will provide' (v. 14). The final section, concluding with the significant words 'because you have obeyed me' (v. 18), reveal the Lord's response to Abraham's faith in this testing time.

So the story begins and concludes with the Lord first testing Abraham, then blessing him. We can see, then, that the whole narrative rests on and enlarges the topic sentence. Here, discovering the topic sentence has encouraged me to look at the Lord in the story, more than at Abraham – and perhaps that's how it should be. Interestingly, the writer to the Hebrews also picks up the topic sentence: 'By faith Abraham, when God tested him...' (11:17). The Old Testament passage certainly seems to put God as central to our reading (see Genesis 22:1, 8, 11, 12, 15–18), and this adds considerable interest to our reflection on the passage.

See for yourself

Take the following passages and read them slowly and thoughtfully, seeking to engage with them rather than simply reading the text. Discover the topic sentence – the one upon which everything else seems to hang. Reflect on what that sentence is saying, ask questions of it and then reflect further on the rest of the passage as we have done above.

- Psalm 23
- Ecclesiastes 12:1–8
- Galatians 5:1–13
- Colossians 3:1–17
- James 5:7–12

Two other straightforward strategies which are very similar to finding the topic sentence are: discovering the big idea and choosing a title. Both are sometimes related to finding the topic sentence, as that sentence might well give you the passage's big idea, title or both. For example, the topic sentence of Genesis 1:1 says, 'In the beginning God created the heavens and the earth.' Everything in Genesis 1 hangs from it or explains it. But, on reflection, you'll also see that this sentence could equally be the big idea of the chapter and, indeed, its title. Similarly, the beginning of Galatians 5, 'It is for freedom that Christ has set us free' (v. 1), is the topic sentence of that section of the letter – it determines the rest; but equally it would work as the big idea or the title for the apostle's writing at that juncture. So let's look at these strategies with this in mind.

14

What's the big idea? Intention in a single sentence

Sometimes it's good to gain an overall impression of what a passage is about. When I taught trainee pastors, I used to tell students that when they preached, they should imagine members of their congregation trying to explain what their sermon was about to someone who hadn't been able to attend church that day. In other words, imagine how they would convey the overall message to someone who asked them what the preacher spoke about. The person asking that question usually doesn't want a detailed rundown of the whole sermon, with all the salient points, illustrations and application; they simply want to know what the big idea was and to get it in one sentence.

We might feel that some biblical passages are just too complicated or detailed to engage with and that in reading the passage in detail we lose sight of the wood for the trees. It might be that Exodus 35:30–40:38, which describes making the tabernacle, is one such passage. (Why not read the passage before you move on?) It's certainly one of those portions of scripture that we feel we'd like to at worst miss out or at best rush through. It's just too detailed an account. The curtains, for example, are said to be 28 cubits long and 4 cubits wide. They're joined together – five curtains and another five – with 50 loops on one curtain and 50 on another, and so on (36:8–13). The passage continues in a similar fashion, describing and numbering the frames of acacia wood (ten cubits long and a half wide, 36:21), the blue curtains, the ark itself, the table, the lampstand, the altar of incense, the altar of burnt offering, the basin (made of bronze, 38:8), the courtyard (100 cubits long by 50 wide, 38:9–13), the materials used, the priestly garments and so on. Here, there is no rush. Everything is particularised and detailed. We can see the point for those making the tabernacle and its several parts, but why is this passage in scripture?

I'm sure that an Old Testament expert could give us a careful account of why things are described in this way, and that's all well and good. The question for us, however, might be, how do we engage with this passage in our personal and individual reading of scripture? Instead of getting entrenched in the detail, we could read the passage and then ask ourselves, what is the big idea? An answer to this question might allow us to reflect on the truth of the passage, not the complicated details of it. It might also help us to discern God's intention.

So we're certainly not excused from reading the passage! But we look at it in a particular way. Having come up with 'the big idea', we can focus on that as we read. We might notice a couple of things that help. First, we notice that the passage begins with the fascinating fact that the Lord has chosen and gifted Bezalel son of Uri with 'wisdom, with understanding, with knowledge and with all kinds of skills – to make artistic designs for work in gold, silver and bronze, to cut and set stones, to work in wood and to engage in all kinds of artistic crafts' (35:31–33); indeed, the Lord has 'filled him with the Spirit of God' (35:31). He has also given him, along with Oholiab son of Ahisamak, 'the ability to teach others' (35:34). The Lord has filled the other craftsmen 'with skill to do all kinds of work' (35:35). In other words, the Lord is involved in the detail! Everything that now follows this introduction has the stamp of God's approval upon it; indeed, he has endowed these men with the gift to imagine, to create and to establish the tabernacle as he wants it to be. That sheds new light on 'boring' detail, doesn't it?

Now, when we look with more interest at the detail, eventually we'll arrive at the final section in which the Lord comes to settle upon the tabernacle that has been constructed so precisely. It says that Moses had finished the work and had done so just as the Lord had commanded (see the remarkable repetition, 40:16, 19, 21, 23, 25, 27, 29, 32). At that juncture, and not before, 'the cloud covered the tent of meeting, and the glory of the Lord filled the tabernacle' (40:34) – so much so that Moses himself could not even enter the place.

Because we've refused to read through this section quickly, because we've sought out the big idea through all the detail, we've come to realise the importance of God in all the detail of this slow-moving narrative. God initiates the work of construction; he endows people with gifts ready to build the tabernacle and to array it with beautiful things; he waits until it is complete before he settles upon it and in it. Perhaps the big idea has to do with God, not the tabernacle as such, after all. And, remember, this is the God who evidently desires to dwell with his people, Israel. This is God-in-relationship: the glorious God with his chosen, though fallen, people.

Why not try to put this down somehow as a 'big idea'? How would you say it?

And don't forget that Bible reading should result in reflection. Can you see where this example is leading? I'm reminded of John's gospel, in which he speaks again of the glorious God in the person of his Son, Jesus, settling with his people – fallen, but chosen. John 1:14 says, 'The Word became flesh and made his dwelling [or 'tabernacled' in the Greek] among us. We have seen his glory...' What a wonderful picture, then, of our redeemer God – in the Old Testament detail of the newly built tabernacle and in the physicality of his Son, Jesus.

See for yourself

Take the following biblical passages and read them once or twice before exploring what might be the big idea that encapsulates the meaning.

- Genesis 3
- Isaiah 6:1–8
- James 4:1–10
- 1 John 3:1–3
- Revelation 11

15

Choosing a title: what is the passage about?

The headings in modern Bibles are not part of the original text but are added by the publisher. Likewise the chapter divisions and verses were inserted later – in the 13th century and mid-16th century, respectively. The original biblical texts were continuous, from beginning to end, without these added reading aids. If we take a look at the headings in Today's New International Version, for example, we'll see that they are generally functional, but do little more than plot a storyline (e.g. 'Crossing the Jordan', Joshua 3) or an argument (e.g. 'Made alive in Christ', Ephesians 2). These are entirely adequate for their purpose, so I'm not going to ask you to reinvent the wheel! Choosing a title as a Bible reading strategy is more creative than that. Let's see very briefly.

Take Acts 4:1—5:11. In this well-known section of Luke's account of the early church, we have four headings in the TNIV: 'Peter and John before the Sanhedrin', 'The believers' prayer', 'The believers share their possessions' and 'Ananias and Sapphira'. Each of these is sufficient for its purpose, but here we're seeking a slightly different end: to think of a title which indicates that we've truly engaged with the *purpose* of the story, that we know and understand what's going on, that we've been biblically attentive.

Read each short passage a couple of times, slowly and thoughtfully. Let's retain the TNIV headings for now, so we know where we are.

Think out loud about what's happening in the passage; ponder it and engage with it in the following manner, if you find it helpful. Then, see if a new, more informed title comes to mind that reflects what you've pondered.

Peter and John before the Sanhedrin. The Sadducees, the priests and the captain of the temple guard are said to be 'greatly disturbed' (4:2) because the apostles, Peter and John are proclaiming Jesus and the resurrection of the dead. This is clearly an important start to the chapter – the dispute is about the proclamation of Jesus Christ. This continues when, on being questioned, Peter asserts that the crippled man was miraculously healed 'by the name of Jesus Christ of Nazareth' (4:10) – indeed, salvation is found in no one else (4:12). We notice, too, that the Sanhedrin's decision hinges on the name of Jesus (4:17) and Peter's declaration that they cannot but preach, having been called by God to do so (4:19–20).

So the rather passive title 'Peter and John before the Sanhedrin' doesn't really do the passage justice, at least in the way we're seeking to engage with it. What would you title this short passage? Are there words you can't do without – like Jesus, proclamation, gospel, courage? What title would get you close to the core of the biblical narrative here?

The believers' prayer. In this short piece the apostles return to the fellowship of believers, recounting their story. This is followed by immediate, bold and fervent prayer. Noticeably, their prayer begins with the thought of who God is, not with the difficult situation they face, however trying that is and however fearful that must have made them. God is the creator of everything; who else would they turn to? He is greater than anything they might have to face (4:24).

Then, quoting the wonderful second psalm that encourages faith in a powerful God (4:25–26), they apply the words to the situation they confront (4:27). Rather than 'using' God to retaliate on their account, their prayer now petitions him to do three things: to consider (to keep in mind) the threats of the Sanhedrin; to give the apostles a renewed boldness; and to heal many in the name of Jesus (4:29–30) – notice how that brings their thinking back to Peter and John's preaching, which they did in Jesus' name. After they pray, the room is shaken and they are all filled with the Holy Spirit, sure signs of God's blessing on their request.

Again, what title would you give this passage? What words would best sum up what's happening here? It is about the believers' prayer (TNIV), but is it about something more significant than that?

The believers share their possessions. Now that you're getting the hang of this, look at this passage in the light of the last two we've explored. What stands out for you? It's more than believers sharing all they had – though that is part of the embryonic church's fellowship in action. Notice, for example, verse 33: 'With great power the apostles continued to testify to the resurrection of the Lord Jesus', and the latter half, 'And God's grace was so powerfully at work in them all'. There's something significant happening here. And, by renaming the biblical sections, we might portray what it is. It has to do with Jesus Christ as absolutely central to the church's message, and the grace and presence of God among them.

Now you could go back and reread the section to see if your headings capture the dynamic (and intention) of Luke in writing the narrative.

- What are your new headings?
- Look back at Jesus' declaration in Acts 1:8: 'But you will receive power when the Holy Spirit comes on you; and you will be my witnesses in Jerusalem, and in all Judea and Samaria, and to the ends of the earth.' Do your new titles fit with what he says? That might encourage you that you've gained a real understanding of Luke's message.
- How is the Lord speaking to you through what you've done on this strategy?

- Finally, read through Acts 5:1–11, the awful story of Ananias and Sapphira, their complicit deception and their unexpected and sudden deaths. The TNIV titles this story nominally, 'Ananias and Sapphira', but how would you now title that section with what you've done so far in mind?

See for yourself

Here are some other biblical passages that you could practise on. Give titles to the following. Remember to read each passage carefully a couple of times, consider it prayerfully until you feel you know what's going on, then give a suitable title.

- Exodus 19
- 1 Kings 19:9–18
- Psalm 51
- Psalm 130
- Matthew 4:12–25
- Luke 7:11–17
- 2 Peter 3

16

Seeing gospel grace: always yes, in Christ

Scripture covers every facet of the believer's life with the Lord – joy, praise, connection, security and so on, as well as grief, despair, detachment and lament. There are individual and communal expressions of these experiences throughout the Bible. From God's perspective, too, there are times of divine rejoicing as well as periods of righteous anger, even judgement. The Psalms are full of the former, for example, and the prophetic writing is replete with the latter. This can be off-putting to our reading of particular portions of the Bible as we feel more and more downcast by the negative side. You have to read a great deal of Ezekiel, for instance, before you reach any intimations of grace.

As a general rule, it's good to keep in mind that the more negative aspects of scripture are important truths about humanity's condition – about our condition – before God. But also remember that they are precursors of the eventual revelation of grace, which becomes dramatically highlighted before such sin. So, as a Bible reading strategy, I would suggest that without sidestepping important truths we shouldn't allow ourselves to get trapped in the negative. It's helpful to look carefully for positive signs. Scripture is ultimately about divine grace, not judgement. The gospel is 'Yes' not 'No' in Jesus Christ. 'For God did not send his Son into the world to condemn the world, but to save the world through him' (John 3:17). Try to see that everywhere you read.

Let's see what this means in practice. We'll look at Jeremiah 14 as a good starting place and then at Psalm 51 to demonstrate this strategy.

Jeremiah 14

As with many of the prophetic writings, Jeremiah's prophecy is a revelation of God's anger against a rebellious and faithless people and its consequent judgement on them. 'I have withdrawn my blessing, my love and my pity from this people,' declares the Lord (Jeremiah 16:5). As such, much of Jeremiah is a difficult read about the destruction of Jerusalem and its inhabitants by foreign invaders fulfilling the will of God against his own covenant people. It's about their shame, disgrace, disobedience and judgement. The prophet is so distraught that he even questions the Lord's faithfulness: 'Is the Lord not in Zion? Is her King no longer there?' (Jeremiah 8:19). It makes for sober reading, and perhaps we might find something of our own faithlessness in its pages, too, and a need to repent and turn back to the Lord. I don't want to sidestep that possible and significant application. However, a careful reading of chapter 14 might give us a helpful reading strategy, for in that chapter we can perhaps see something of our own reaction.

The picture is painted in graphic words:

> Judah mourns,
>   her cities languish;
> they wail for the land,
>   and a cry goes up from Jerusalem.
> JEREMIAH 14:2

There is drought; people are despairing; the prophet admits their guilt and their shame; the Lord threatens to destroy his people 'with the sword, famine and plague' (Jeremiah 14:12). He rejects them out of hand. How are we to read this passage and indeed other similarly distressing portions of Jeremiah and other prophetic writings? This is where the helpful distinction between reading and listening (Eugene Peterson; see p. 30), or reading and engaging, is useful. I say with some shame that I've read such passages all my life simply at face value. I've taken it that Israel or Judah have deserved what they got and that the Lord has every right to do as he pleases with his people (see Jeremiah 18). And I've generally read with interest, but without real profit and with no sense of godly indignation. And it's this last phrase that gives us a clue to engaging with such passages.

What is Jeremiah's response to what is happening? Jeremiah is indignant! Read these verses slowly through:

> Although our sins testify against us,
>> do something, Lord, for the sake of your name.
> For our backsliding is great;
>> we have sinned against you.
> You who are the hope of Israel,
>> its Saviour in times of distress,
> why are you like a stranger in the land,
>> like a traveller who stays only at night?
> Why are you like someone taken by surprise,
>> like a warrior powerless to save?
> You are among us, Lord,
>> and we bear your name;
>> do not forsake us!
>
> JEREMIAH 14:7–9

Notice that the prophet acknowledges the people's sin and backsliding – including his own. So there's no sense of minimising their faithlessness, as if the Lord has the whole thing wrong and out of proportion. They deserve what they get! However, the prophet doesn't leave it at that. He looks for signs of grace to overcome the judgement. God is 'the hope of Israel' and 'its Saviour in times of distress'. He is among the people even now; they bear his name. And so he feels he can complain at the Lord's apparent absence, and he can plead with him: 'Do something, Lord, for the sake of your name' (v. 7); 'Do not forsake us!' (v. 9). Again, later in the chapter, we read: 'For the sake of your name do not despise us; do not dishonour your glorious throne. Remember your covenant with us and do not break it' (v. 21). And, finally, the ultimate assurance, even in this situation, 'Therefore our hope is in you' (v. 22).

What would our reading of the more negative passages of the prophets, for example, be like if we adopted a similar reading of the situation? Engaging with the prophetic message would mean that we always acknowledged that sin deserves discipline, that the Lord has every right to deal with his wayward people in that way. But in engaging with the prophetic message we would be always looking for intimations and hints of grace, even when they're difficult to find and even if that means questioning the text itself as we read. God is their God; he loves them and has covenanted with them to be their God and for them to be his people. Why won't he help them? Indeed, will he help them? Will he redeem them? Are there signs that he is present – even among the ruins (Micah 3:12)? Question God in and through the text for signs of grace, for signs that punishment is not the ultimate experience of his people, but that grace will be. If this is not obvious in the passage you're reading, read on until you find it – at the end of the day, divine revelation is about grace. Don't get trapped in the negative. Look for signs of Jesus' coming, too (Isaiah 11, for example) – the ultimate indication of the grace of God!

See for yourself

Try engaging with the following passages in a similar way – finding grace and God's love.

- Isaiah 5:1–7
- Jeremiah 16:1–15
- Hosea 6
- Haggai 2:10–19

Psalm 51

This is a well-known psalm of confession – perhaps one of the best known of David's collection. It's a penitential psalm in which David acknowledges his sin before an all-seeing God and asks for restoration. It's easy to read this psalm and to get trapped in the negative side of it – the sinfulness of David and by extension everyone else (v. 5), the confessional aspect of it (vv. 3–4) and the sheer impossibility of self-improvement (v. 7 onwards). Now, let's engage with this text looking for signs of grace.

First, we must acknowledge that it *is* a psalm of confession. David does come to the Lord in shame and guilt and openly confesses his own specific failure. We certainly don't want to sidestep that aspect of the psalm. The Lord might well use it to convict us of our own shortcomings before him, and we should be open to that. David admits knowing his own sin, using three images to convey his sense of having wronged God (vv. 1–2): 'transgressions' refers to a wilful, self-assertive defiance of God, the equivalent of rebellion; 'iniquity' suggests bending or twisting something that was straight, a distortion of something, perhaps a deviation from the right track, putting something out of shape; 'sin' indicates missing the mark, through choice or failure.

A good look at these images indicates that David is not so much speaking about breaking the law, but about distorting his relationship with the Lord. He underlines this, saying, 'Against you, you only, have I sinned' (v. 4). The aspect of the situation that troubles him more than anything is losing the friendship of God, losing his closeness to the Lord. David longs for reality, a clear relationship with his God. The first line says, 'Have mercy on me, O God!' This is a word of pleading, from sinful David to the righteous God, or from a child of God to the Father.

So, as I say, we need to acknowledge the 'negative' aspect of the psalm – the sinfulness of its writer and his heartfelt confession of that sin. But is that what the psalm is about? As we engage with it, looking for grace, we find that it isn't! Confession is a very personal and private thing. Yet, this personal psalm has become a communal one; this private confession is given to millions of people reading the Hebrew scriptures or the Old Testament. It has been recited by whole communities. Why is that? It is because generations upon generations have seen divine grace writ large in its verses, rather than the sin that initiates David's private but very public song.

The psalm begins with an acknowledgement that God's goodness is demonstrated in the forgiveness of sin. The first verse indicates as much:

> Have mercy on me, O God,
>   according to your unfailing love;
> according to your great compassion
>   blot out my transgressions.
> PSALM 51:1

He calls upon God to act and to do so on the basis of who he's proven himself to be: a God of unfailing love and great compassion. David offers nothing; he has nothing to bargain with; he is empty-handed before a God rich in love. Importantly, David recognises that it is God's initiative alone that can restore his relationship. Notice the imperative verbs and images that seem to suggest this: 'have mercy', 'blot out' (erasing words from a scroll or a tablet, or cancelling the debt from a ledger), 'wash away' (pummelling clothes in a river, beating them on a rock to eradicate every bit of dirt), 'cleanse' (taking unwanted dross from metal in the furnace to make it pure). But it is God's doing, God's activity, that David calls for, not his own effort. He is sure that only the gracious activity of God (the God he has wronged, remember) can bring forgiveness and new life.

These imperatives continue throughout much of the psalm. They come with confidence, not diffidence:

> *Cleanse me with hyssop*, and I shall be clean;
>   *wash me*, and I will be whiter than snow.
>
> PSALM 51:7 (emphasis added)

Imperatives keep coming, demonstrating David's trust in the Lord's ability, intention and goodness: 'Hide your face from my sins' (v. 9), 'Create in me', 'renew' (v. 10), 'Restore to me' (v. 12), 'Deliver me' (v. 14), 'Open my lips' (v. 15). Right at the centre of the psalm is verse 10. The TNIV translates this important verse as follows: 'Create in me a pure heart, O God.' As so often, Eugene Peterson puts his finger on the significance of this in his translation:

> God, make a fresh start in me,
>   shape a Genesis week from the chaos of my life.
>
> PSALM 51:10 (MSG)

David pleads with the Lord, the creator, to start again with him, to begin again on a clean page, to bring order and goodness out of the chaos of his sinful life, just as he did at creation itself. He trusts that God will claim his life again and re-establish its divine purpose. This is the psalmist petitioning for creative grace.

See for yourself

Do you see how, when we look for signs of grace, we find a whole new reading of Psalm 51? It is about sin and confession; but it is also (and more so) about the grace of God, even in a dire personal situation of sin and faithlessness. Look for grace! Try looking for grace in the following passages:

- Psalm 28
- Psalm 53
- Psalm 71

17

The slow way: verse by verse

Sometimes it's a good idea to take each verse at a time and to concentrate on exactly what is happening or what is being said. This takes time, but it can reap clear dividends and ensure a detailed focus on the text of scripture you're seeking to engage with. It's important, again, to do this prayerfully – asking the Lord to show you his intention, his will and his truth and to apply that to your present circumstances. Let's look at a couple of short passages in this way and see how it works: first, Luke 9:18–27; then, John 13:1–17.

Luke 9:18–27

This is a pivotal passage in Luke's gospel narrative, being the first time that one of Jesus' disciples recognises him as the Messiah and calls him such. The conversation draws that declaration from Peter in this instance. A thoughtful reading of each verse will be useful after prayerfully reading the whole passage a couple of times through.

Verse 18. It's interesting that Jesus prays in private, with his disciples. On other occasions he leaves his disciples and prays alone. Having read through the whole passage, though, I realise this isn't what it's about – important as it is. He asks them a question, seeking *their* understanding of who he is: 'Who do the crowds say I am?'

Verse 19. The as-yet uncommitted masses think Jesus could be the resurrected John the Baptist, the Old Testament prophet Elijah or another prophet. I'm not going to follow these suggestions through, as they have elements of both tradition and superstition about them. However we read these, the point is that they woefully fall short of the truth about Jesus.

Verse 20. Jesus asks for the disciples' response. Is this a contrast between the crowds and the followers of Jesus to indicate that the question is not simply historical or theological but personal, relational? 'Who do you say I am?' Peter affirms his faith in Jesus, though it's doubtful he knows the fullness of what he's confessed.

Verse 21. Jesus warns them to keep this truth to themselves for the time being.

Verse 22. Jesus spells out the implications for himself: as Messiah, he will suffer rejection by God's own people, he will be killed, but on the third day he'll be 'raised to life'. So, for Jesus, being Messiah (God's anointed one) means being obedient through suffering to triumph.

Verses 23–24. Here are enigmatic sayings to indicate that discipleship is also about obedience, about suffering (self-denial, taking up a cross), about putting the kingdom of God first, before everything else.

Verses 25–27. Jesus asks a rhetorical question: 'What good is it for you to gain the whole world, and yet lose or forfeit your very self?' and reminds them in stark terms that they are going to become unashamed witnesses of Jesus, the Son of Man, even to death.

So, having thought about each verse, what have we learned from this engagement with scripture? It's good to stop and to reflect on this, even briefly. We've noticed that there is a contrast between the crowd's view of Jesus and the disciples' view (at least as Peter speaks for them all). When Jesus asks us who we think he is, he's asking for a faith-filled response, a relationship, a spiritual confession. We've also seen that Jesus asks his disciples (and us), on the strength of that response, to follow him, to live with a heightened sense of what really matters in life, to depend on him, being called to witness to who he is and somehow to reflect his life of obedience through suffering to resurrection. Paul's words come to mind:

> I want to know Christ – yes, to know the power of his resurrection and participation in his sufferings, becoming like him in his death, and so, somehow, attaining to the resurrection from the dead.
>
> PHILIPPIANS 3:10–11

John 13:1–17

The beginning of John 13 presents us with an extraordinary passage in which Jesus washes his disciples' feet. Let's look at this in a similar manner.

Verse 1. The setting is important. This event takes place 'just before the Passover Feast' – a time of celebration of the Lord's goodness, of remembering redemption, freedom from slavery, new life and the blessing of community. Jesus 'knew that the hour had come to leave this world and go to the Father'; he had that insight, that foreknowledge that the end was near. Leaving this world indicates suffering and death; going to the Father implies faithfulness, triumph and eternal welcome. Jesus has done what was asked of him: he had loved his followers right up to the end.[66]

Verse 2. John's comment about Judas being tempted by the devil and his betrayal of Jesus is very significant, because 'the evening meal was in progress'. In other words, Judas and Jesus are sitting at the same table. Whatever happens after this (vv. 4–17) happens with Judas in their midst, and whatever happens after this verse happens to Judas too, including the eating and the foot-washing.

Verse 3. The words 'Jesus knew' give a sense of conviction and of certainty: he knows 'the Father had put all things under his power', and he knows 'that he had come from God' and was about to return to God. He knows that; he is certain of it.

Verses 4–5. The translation I have begins with the word 'so' – Jesus knows he has been given all power, he knows he's returning to God, *so* (therefore) he wraps a towel around himself, pours water into a basin and washes his disciples' feet (even those of Judas). Reflecting on his own glory and on his soon-to-be triumphant return to the presence of the Father, he becomes a servant figure at the meal. It was customary for servants to wash feet made dirty by the sandy and unsanitary streets. On occasion wives would undertake the very menial task (see, for example, 1 Samuel 25:41). But it was always undertaken by the inferior for the superior (given the social hierarchy of the day). But here is Jesus, washing his disciples' dirty feet.

Verses 6–9. No wonder Peter protests! Jesus is the host at the meal; he should not be washing their feet. But the disciple has misunderstood the prophetic significance of what Jesus is doing: 'Unless I wash you, you have no part with me' (v. 8). So foot-washing has something to do with having a part with Christ. If that's the case, Peter dives straight in (v. 9).

Verses 10–11. Jesus acknowledges Judas' presence and his coming betrayal. He also indicates that having a part with Jesus has to do with being 'clean'.

Verses 12–17. Jesus resumes his position as Lord and teacher. If their teacher washes their feet, they should do likewise. Jesus is speaking of the necessity of following him in humility – a humility that does not take people's supposed status into account.

The first three verses invite us to read the whole passage in the light of the cross – the Passover, the hour had come, leaving the world, he loved them to the end. Perhaps the words 'Unless I wash you,

you have no part with me' (v. 8) imply both a relationship with the humble Christ and a portion, an inheritance with him, too. Also, because of the obvious and gracious hospitality displayed by Jesus, the passage reminds us of his welcome to all, no matter who they are, into his kingdom. The guest needs to accept and to receive the grace offered (v. 9), then to embody and offer that grace to others (v. 14). There is a gracious inclusivity here for those who are humble enough to accept the kingdom.

See for yourself

Do you see how reading verse by verse and reflecting upon them can help us to engage with what the passage has to offer? Why not try the strategy with the following passages:

- Exodus 17:1–7
- Proverbs 30:1–9
- Matthew 3:1–12
- Galatians 3:1–5
- 2 Peter 3

Part IV

Things to take into account when reading the text

As we read through scripture there are several things to notice, things to take into account that will inform our understanding and our thoughtful engagement. In this part we look at some of these. They are not in themselves reading strategies, but remembering them will certainly help our Bible reading.

18

Poetic licence: daring to speak of God

As we read the Bible we need to remember two important things: first, that words are woefully inadequate to describe the awesome God; and second, that words are all we have to do so with.

When we reflect on this, we realise that we cannot imagine God, let alone speak with any confidence about him. Our human and fallen thinking is altogether too limited, even at its most profound. 'How great is God – beyond our understanding!' declares Job's friend, Elihu (Job 36:26). Theologians, therefore, through many generations have spoken of the incomprehensibility of God: he is simply incomprehensible (unfathomable, inconceivable) to us. That's not to say we know nothing; in his grace, the Lord has revealed himself through history to many individuals and nations, particularly Israel. But those receiving revelation have found the inadequacy of words, even as they write scripture. It's worth remembering this as we read the Bible.

Ezekiel 1

Let's look at an example of what I mean. Ezekiel is a powerful book of the Bible, but it is a difficult read, with all its prophecies against surrounding nations, its laments and its warnings, with positive salvific content coming rather late in the book (from chapter 34 onwards). It's also difficult because of its depiction of God himself, and the prophet is surely conscious of this. As we read chapter 1, we become aware of it too.

Ezekiel begins his prophecy by trying to describe what he saw in a vision when 'the heavens were opened' (1:1). He sees 'a violent storm coming out of the north – an immense cloud with flashing lightning and surrounded by brilliant light' (v. 4). Already we sense his grasping for appropriate vocabulary, a way to describe the inexpressible. The rest of chapter 1 is worth reading for its complexity: fire, living creatures, movement, flashes of lightning, wheels, eyes, roaring and so on. Just pause for a moment and read this passage (vv. 4–24).

I don't think we have an exact representation of what the prophet saw. Rather he gives us an *impression* of movement, light, noise, majesty and holiness. He writes as an impressionist with colour and vigorous texture, rather than as a graphic artist with pen and ink. From verse 24 Ezekiel begins to say something about God himself: the roar of his voice ('like the roar of rushing waters… like the tumult of an army'), a throne, a figure 'like that of a man' (but full of fire, like glowing metal) and brilliant light surrounding him: 'Like the appearance of a rainbow in the clouds on a rainy day, so was the radiance around him' (v. 28). We can sense words and images failing the prophet as he seeks to describe that which is beyond words, but not beyond experience. Indeed, Christopher Wright, an Old Testament specialist, speaks of Ezekiel's language here: 'This account is full of hasty, disjointed and ungrammatical language, tumbling along as words struggle to cope with an overwhelmingly awesome confrontation with the majesty of God.'[67]

Ezekiel's conclusion is that 'this was the appearance of the likeness of the glory of the Lord' (v. 28). No wonder he falls fearfully flat on his face before such majesty! And it's not entirely surprising that throughout his prophecy he seems to use the short-hand phrase 'the glory of the Lord' to conjure up this whole unfathomable sight time and time again (see, for example, 3:23; 8:4).

If the authors of biblical books find it terribly difficult – nearly impossible – to describe the God who speaks to them, then on reading scripture we shouldn't be dismayed that we sometimes can't picture what they are saying to us. If they struggled with the original revelation, how much more will we with the imperfect representation of it?

As an aside, I find this a significant thought in my reading of the book of Revelation. I usually attempt to read this straight through, from beginning to end (pausing only at 8:1, 'When he opened the seventh seal, there was silence in heaven for about half an hour'). Mostly, it's the impression that I read to gain – the movement, the conflict, the triumph, the new heavens and earth, and so on. There are other opportunities to read more carefully and with others' help.

Psalm 36:5–10

It's not just prophets who find it difficult to describe the Lord. In a different way, the psalmist in Psalm 36, for instance, has to employ somewhat contorted language to picture the love of God – which in its fullness is simply beyond human description. He finds that language isn't nearly grand enough for the task. It soon reaches its limits as he seeks to worship the Lord and to plead the cause of his people. So in a series of images the psalmist goes further than literal language can: God's love 'reaches to the heavens', his faithfulness 'to the skies'; his 'righteousness is like the highest mountains', his justice 'like the great deep'; the Lord's love is 'priceless'; in his light 'we see light' (vv. 5–9). It's interesting, though, that the psalmist's grappling with what God is like – his love, faithfulness, righteousness and justice – comes from the concrete familiarity of God in lived experience, for he preserves both animals and human beings (v. 6), protects people (v. 7), is generous (v. 8) and is life and light (v. 9).

As Ezekiel struggles with language to speak for God about God, so the psalmist struggles with it to speak of God to God. The problem is similar. How far can language take us in these pursuits? When we read scripture, we might benefit from remembering the difficulty of language's inadequacy in the face of the living God, for those who dare to speak of him to us.

Before we move on, we should remember that, while we cannot imagine or conceive of God, we have 'the exact representation' of God and 'the radiance of God's glory' in Jesus Christ (Hebrews 1:3). If we want to know what God is like, then we need go no further than looking at the person of Jesus. He is the true icon (*eikōn* in Greek: image, likeness) of God (see John 14:7, Colossians 1:15).

See for yourself

Look at the following passages and see what you make of the language which attempts to convey God's person and presence.

- Exodus 19:16–19
- Exodus 40:34–35
- Job 38—41
- Isaiah 6:1–9
- Ezekiel 43:1–5
- Daniel 7:13–14
- Revelation 1:12–18

19

Poetic language: the imagery of faith

As we've seen in the previous chapter, the writers of scripture use imagery to express their faith, especially when they attempt to speak of God. However, the thing to remember about imagery is that it isn't always wholly synonymous with what it describes. To take a well-worn example, to say that someone walked as slow as a snail describes the slowness of his movement but nothing more than that. You can't deduce more from that simile; nor should you take it literally. It simply tells you one thing, and that is about the person's slowness of pace.

So the biblical imagery of God sitting on a throne (see, for example, Isaiah 6) suggests that he has authority and rule, and it automatically triggers a stark contrast with earthly kings. It does not mean that he literally sits on a throne. The Lord as a shepherd (Psalm 23) brings to mind his protection, provision, care and leading, not that he actually herds sheep. Similarly, the Lord as a rock and a fortress (Psalm 18) must not be taken too literally. They tell us significant things about the nature of God's care in language we can understand.

In his really helpful guide to the Psalms, Simon Stocks suggests the following as things to look out for when reading that particular book of the Old Testament:[68]

- A 'way' or a 'path' denotes lifestyle, especially the decisions that are made about how to live in relation to other people (e.g. 1:1, 6).

- 'Trees' often represent life, growth and fruitfulness – the production of something good and nourishing (1:3; 92:12–15).

- 'Water' can have opposing connotations: either something nourishing and life-giving, usually when denoted as 'river' or 'dew' (36:8), or something threatening and chaotic, when denoted as 'sea' or 'deep' (65:7).

- 'Leviathan' and 'Rahab' are mythical creatures that represent evil or chaos and that dwell in the sea (74:14; 89:10).

- A 'rock' is often a symbol of strength and security (19:14). In contrast, the 'earth shaking' represents calamity or serious threat, much as we might speak today of an 'earth-shattering event' (82:5).

- A 'trap' or 'snare' represents a situation that is sinister or malicious and threatening or harmful (124:7). In contrast, safety and goodwill are found in a 'refuge' (14:6).

- Safety and security are also denoted by being 'in the shadow of God's wings', which draws upon the image of a bird protecting her young close to her body (17:8).

- Perhaps most fundamentally of all, 'up' and 'high' represent better/happier/more valuable/more alive, while 'down' and 'low' are the opposites (113:4; 116:6).

These are good examples to look out for throughout the Old Testament, not just in the Psalms, and there are plenty of others. The authors of the New Testament use imagery too. The apostle Paul grapples with a living and diverse theology of the church that does justice to what he sees happening in those nascent groups of men and women, and he employs the image of a body made up of different parts to do so (1 Corinthians 12:12–31). He struggles to grasp a theology of resurrection and uses the image of seeds to explain the unexplainable (1 Corinthians 15:42–44). Similarly, Peter employs Old Testament imagery – stones and the cornerstone, priests and so on – to speak of the church and its relationship with Christ (1 Peter 2:4–8, 9).

So look out for the use of imagery in the books you read from scripture. Recognise images for what they are – limited and pictorial representations that emphasise one or two things about their subject. Don't take them literally; read from them, not into them.

That last point is worth labouring a little. Several years ago, I was at a group discussing scripture, and our small group of six or seven people was asked to consider a couple of verses from Isaiah:

> Yet you, Lord, are our Father.
>   We are the clay, you are the potter;
>   we are all the work of your hand.
> Do not be angry beyond measure, Lord;
>   do not remember our sins forever.
> Oh, look up on us we pray,
>   for we are all your people.
> ISAIAH 64:8–9

The passage is a superb example of biblical imagery. It begins with the image of God as a father, then turns to consider his relationship with his people as a potter with the clay. The images come in the context of the sinfulness of his people, and the writer therefore reminds God that he has a special relationship with his people – he is their Father; he created them, made them; they are the work of his hands. In the group we were asked to share what this image said to us. The person who first offered a suggestion said that it reminded him that the Lord and he were dancers and that they danced together, the Lord holding him closely as they did so. Now, as hard as

I tried, I just couldn't square that conclusion with the text, which had something very different to say to us. This person's interpretation read *into* the image, not *from* it. It's best to stick to the text. What does the image imply? What does it say?

See for yourself

Why not try this for yourself? Look at the following passages and consider the images in them. What do they convey? How is this helpful to your understanding?

- Psalm 102:1–12
- Psalm 119:105–112
- Isaiah 40:11
- Matthew 13:31–33
- Ephesians 2:19–22
- Colossians 3:1–14

20

God-focused: Trinitarian shape

The Christian faith has as its foundational creedal assertion a belief in one God, three persons – Father, Son and Holy Spirit. It's a difficult teaching to elucidate, and it's not our task to do so here. In fact, the doctrine is not found explicitly in either the Old or the New Testament, but it *is* implied in the New and from that we may deduce it in the Old. Theologians have been trying to work it out ever since the New Testament writers grappled with who God is. We can leave that to them! In reading scripture, however, it's good to engage with the text with a focus on God, as I've said before. Again, Eugene Peterson is extremely helpful on this, seeing the complementarity of the situation:

> The authorial character of the Holy Scriptures was established as personal in the persons of Father, Son, and Holy Spirit. Because it was personal it was also relational... This was accompanied by the realization that these Holy Scriptures, in which God was revealing everything of who God is, also included everything of who we are: there is comprehensiveness and personal participation on both sides, author and reader.

He continues with some emphasis:

> This may be the single most important thing to know as we come to read and study and believe these Holy Scriptures: this

rich, alive, personally revealing God as experienced in Father, Son, and Holy Spirit, personally addressing us in whatever circumstances we find ourselves…[69]

This is important. If scripture reveals God to us, it reveals God the Father, Son and Holy Spirit. We would surely truncate our biblical engagement if we ignored this fact in the text. In this context, notice the following passage from the apostle Paul:

And you also were included in Christ when you heard the word of truth, the gospel of your salvation. When you believed you were marked in him with a seal, the promised Holy Spirit, who is a deposit guaranteeing our inheritance until the redemption of those who are God's possession – to the praise of his glory.
EPHESIANS 1:13–14

The shape that Paul creates here is important. Notice, first, the words 'included', 'believed', 'until the redemption of those'. These imply the beginning and the end of Christian experience; they outline in brief the believer's life and experience of God. But the apostle also shapes his thinking with the Trinity in mind: 'included in Christ' (the Son), 'the promised Holy Spirit', 'God's possession' (the Father). He does this again a little later: 'And in him [Jesus Christ] you too are being built together to become a dwelling in which God [the Father] lives by his Spirit' (Ephesians 2:22).

It's important for us to read the Bible with the Trinity in mind. Not only is God somehow the author of this wonderful book, but he is also the author of our salvation – a salvation granted to fallen human beings by the grace of God through Jesus Christ and by the Holy Spirit. The Lord is central to the narrative, then: as I've said before, not Israel, not the church, not us, but God. It helps tremendously if we keep that in mind as we read scripture. This works itself out if generally we look first at what can be learned about God, then about ourselves.

See for yourself

Why not look for intimations of the Trinity – that is, of God – throughout scripture? Look at the following passages, for example.

- Mark 1:9–13
- John 1:1–18
- Romans 1:1–7
- Galatians 3:1–5
- Colossians 1:3–8

And in the light of what you've discovered in these, and perhaps other passages, why not delve into the Old Testament to see God revealed there, too?

- Genesis 1:1
- Ezekiel 37:1–14
- Joel 2:28–32

21

When things are difficult: theology and experience

There are texts of scripture that display a disjunction between the believer's theology or understanding and their experience. How are we to read these, engage with them and learn from them?

Psalm 22 and Job 19

The psalmist's cry in Psalm 22 is a perfect example: 'My God, my God, why have you forsaken me? Why are you so far from saving me, so far from the words of my groaning?' (v. 1). The book of Job has examples of similarly apparent discrepancies between experience and known truth about God: 'Then know that God has wronged me and drawn his net around me' (19:6). Reading these passages and others raises questions that seem difficult to answer: does God really forsake his covenant people? Does he wrong his servants, as Job suggests? Is God ever our enemy? It's here that we need to be wise about our engagement with the biblical text. We mustn't take these verses, these thoughts, out of the mitigating circumstances in which we find them. And we shouldn't remain in the negative comments, but search for a more positive conclusion, if we can discern one.

If we read the whole of Psalm 22, we find that the psalmist is for some undisclosed reason in deep conflict with everyone around him:

'scorned by everyone, despised by the people' (v. 6), mocked and insulted (v. 7). Perhaps those who scorn see the very discrepancy that we observe (v. 8). He fears to the extent that he has physical symptoms: his bones feel out of joint, his heart is melting, his mouth is dry, his tongue sticks to the roof of his mouth (vv. 14–15) and so on. The situation seems so difficult to him that he feels as though the Lord has forsaken him entirely (v. 1). He cries out in desperation and anguish.

We can ourselves empathise with his plight and with his words. But the forsakenness of God is not his conclusion on the matter, nor is it a doctrine of scripture. His conclusion is rather different, and he moves slowly towards that conclusion by remembering that his ancestors trusted God entirely (v. 4) and were saved (v. 5). He reminds himself that the Lord has been his God from birth (v. 10), that he is his strength (v. 19), and concludes with the assurance that one day the whole earth will praise his God (vv. 27–31). So, though we can certainly empathise with the psalmist for his anguish and lament, we need to stay with his developing thought to the point of those last confident words about God: 'They will proclaim his righteousness, declaring to a people yet unborn: he has done it!' (v. 31).

Job is similar, but more expansive. His circumstances are well known – calamity upon calamity, distress upon distress, taking his family and his prosperity and eventually his health too. Listening to his friends attempting to explain the situation with little success or sensitivity, he cries out that God has wronged him (19:6), that he has 'shrouded [his] paths in darkness' (v. 8), that he angrily counts him as an enemy (v. 11). And yet, amid this painful diatribe, he speaks these unfathomably profound words:

I know that my redeemer lives,
    and that in the end he will stand on the earth.
And after my skin has been destroyed,
    yet in my flesh I will see God;

I myself will see him
 with my own eyes – I, and not another.
 How my heart yearns within me!

JOB 19:25–27

Anyone who has read the whole book of Job will know that uttering these words, as magnificent as they are, is not the point at which Job finally finds peace or assurance. We have to wait another 23 gruelling chapters to reach that – and it remarkably mirrors his comment here: 'My ears had heard of you but now my eyes have seen you' (42:5). But even here in chapter 19 we glimpse something other than simply lament and anguish. We see in Job a faith that reaches beyond his circumstances to a trust in a God who at present seems either absent or, worse, actively against him.

Lamentations 3:19–32

To see this text in context, why not read Lamentations at this point? It's reasonably short! The mitigating circumstance for this passage (3:19–32) is truly devastating: the destruction of Jerusalem, the brutal exile of many of its inhabitants and the ongoing hardships that the people who remained faced day upon day. Lamentations is a grim book. Jeremiah, its author, laments, 'How deserted lies the city, once so full of people!' (1:1). Jerusalem has been destroyed by enemies and seemingly abandoned by God; she sits like a grieving widow. Young men and women have been taken, the city is in ruins, starving children beg for bread from their mothers, starving mothers are turned to cannibalism, women are raped, worship of God has disappeared – Jerusalem's 'wound is as deep as the sea' (2:13). And the worst aspect of this situation is that it is the Lord's doing, his punishment for a rebellious people (see chapter 2). This is where 3:19–32 fits in. The prophet, crushed and broken, pictures himself in the darkness of despair; he feels like a besieged city, a laughing stock – vulnerable, homeless, forgotten and rejected by God.

The writer's soul is downcast within him (v. 20). He seems to be brooding on that, even agonising over it. The fact that it's his 'soul' that is low seems to add weight to this – it seems the whole of his being is affected by sorrow, bitterness and grief. He speaks of the Lord bringing this grief upon him (v. 32). His pain and distress are intolerable. The first two verses (vv. 19–20) spell out the grief, vulnerability, rejection and loss of peace, all of which consume the man – graphically, he feels 'cast off' (v. 31). This last phrase is particularly vivid, pointing as it does to feeling thrown aside, not simply abandoned, by God.

This brings us to the seeming contrast between experience and understanding or theology. The writer, amid these grave difficulties, reminds himself that God is loving towards him despite his awful present circumstances. In this amazing short passage (3:19–32) he speaks of 'the Lord's great love' (v. 22), his goodness, his compassion and his faithfulness. It seems that faith looks beyond present circumstances and believes that God is always for us. Here is a godly man who grieves and laments, weary, troubled and humiliated, distressed and suffering – crushed and heartbroken – in a situation in which everything is fractured and out of joint; a man who in these dire circumstances remembers that God is faithful, trustworthy and reliable.

Two phrases stand out here – and they are very instructive for our biblical engagement. The first is in verse 21, where Jeremiah says, 'Yet this I call to mind.' Here is a conscious decision in the context of distress: he decides to bring to the fore, to consciously remember. He digs around in the memories of his own experience and that of his people and concludes that God has always been faithful, and he puts his trust and hope in that same faithfulness of God even now. The second phrase that stands out is 'The Lord is my portion' (v. 24). It's significant that both these phrases are followed by 'therefore': 'Yet this I call to mind and *therefore* I have hope' (v. 21); 'The Lord is my portion; *therefore* I will wait for him' (v. 24). *Because* the Lord's 'compassions never fail' (v. 22), *because* they are 'new every morning' (v. 23), the writer has hope and he waits for the Lord's presence. He knows that 'the Lord is good to those whose hope is in him' (v. 25), that those who wait quietly for salvation will see the goodness of God (v. 26).

The psalmist, Job and Jeremiah the prophet, then, can teach us something about reading scripture and our biblical engagement. When we read passages like the ones we've just considered – passages where the circumstances and the theology seem at first to be so disjointed – there are a few things that would be good to remember.

- First, take to heart the situation in which the writer laments – feel it with them, see it, realise its harshness and difficulty. This will remind us that these writers are like us: human, fragile and sometimes in a difficult place. They may even blame God for the mess and lament his absence, as we've seen.

- Second, try to work through the writer's initial emotions towards their more positive appraisal. This is easier with some than with others – Jeremiah in Lamentations is a case in point, perhaps. If you keep reading, almost inevitably you'll come to the point at which the writer turns again to the Lord in trust and quiet.

- Third, because biblical engagement is about how we consequently live, as well as how we read, don't feel that these examples and others encourage us to moan at God, blaming him for the situation which we presently face. On the one hand, they do convince us to be ourselves, to be entirely open with God, reacting to distressing circumstances as we are; but on the other hand they also encourage us to look for a more positive way – the way of trust and confidence in the continuing love and grace of God in *every* circumstance.

See for yourself

Read the following passages and consider what we've been saying here:

- Psalm 38
- Psalm 80
- Isaiah 37
- Habakkuk 1—2

22

Rhetorical questions: should I answer them?

A rhetorical question is one asked for a dramatic effect or to make a point, not to elicit an answer, and we find them in the Bible doing just that. For example, if you read Job 38—41 you'll find at least 71 rhetorical questions (in the NIV) – questions asked of Job by God, questions as profound as 'Who then is able to stand against me?' (41:10) and as seemingly mundane as 'Do you know when the mountain goats give birth?' (39:1). Here, given the chapters that have preceded this section, rhetorical questions are employed to encourage Job to realise just who God is and who he himself is in comparison. Job's response suggests this:

Then Job answered the Lord:
'I am unworthy – how can I reply to you?
    I put my hand over my mouth.
I spoke once, but I have no answer –
    twice, but I will say no more.'
JOB 40:3–5

So here, in the context of the profound wisdom of the book of Job, rhetorical questions come not so much as implied criticism, but rather as prompts deepening our faith to see a greater God than we can ever imagine.[70] Rhetorical questions become powerful teaching aids in scripture.

The prophet Isaiah employs rhetorical questions in a similar way. Isaiah 40 repeats the same question twice. 'With whom, then, will you compare God?' the prophet asks (40:18). The force of this question is heightened by the fact that the second time it's the Lord himself asking: 'To whom will you compare me?' (40:25). The second enquiry is preceded by the following robust passage, including some more rhetorical questions for emphasis:

> Do you not know?
>   Have you not heard?
> Has it not been told you from the beginning?
>   Have you not understood since the earth was founded?
> He sits enthroned above the circle of the earth,
>   and its people are like grasshoppers...
> 'To whom will you compare me?
>   Or who is my equal?' says the Holy One.
> ISAIAH 40:21–22, 25

Similarly, in the New Testament, the apostle Paul sometimes uses rhetorical questions. Galatians 3:1–5 is an example. In a very short passage, berating the members of the Galatian church for the way they have begun trusting in themselves rather than in Jesus Christ (see 5:4), he asks six rhetorical questions, one after the other:

- Who has bewitched you?
- Did you receive the Spirit by observing the law, or by believing what you heard?
- Are you so foolish?
- After beginning with the Spirit, are you now trying to finish by human effort?
- Have you experienced so much in vain – if it really was in vain?
- Does God give you his Spirit and work miracles among you by your observing the law, or by your believing what you heard?

He clearly doesn't need an answer to any of these questions. Those who heard these questions from the apostle must have felt bombarded by them – six body blows to their self-confidence and behaviour; six piercing criticisms of the inadequacy of their present faith experience. Paul asks rhetorical questions not because he requires them to answer, but to encourage those who hear to look behind them to the absurdity of their own situation in which they have all but forsaken Christ to go their own way (5:2, 4), encouraged by those who have infiltrated their ranks (see 1:6–9; 5:10).

Rhetorical questions, then, can make a point, make a profound criticism, explain or prompt thought. They are used throughout the Bible by writers and characters alike. When we come across them, we might just pause a moment to ask what these might have meant in the original context, and what they say or imply to us today.

See for yourself

Why not look at the following and consider the rhetorical questions in them? (That's not a rhetorical question!)

- Isaiah 44:19
- Jeremiah 13:23; 18:14
- Romans 3:1–9
- Romans 6:1
- Romans 8:33

23

I'll say that again: repetition and meaning

Anyone who has read anything of the Bible will probably know that it is full of repetition – repeated phrases, stories, characters and themes.[71] That shouldn't surprise us, as repetition is a rhetorical device for getting a point across or for making us pause to consider – preachers know that, as do parents and teachers. Repeat something well, and those listening are more likely to take notice. The biblical writers want their readers to engage with what they have to say and therefore they employ repetition liberally. When we read the Bible we need to take repetition seriously, to consider why it's there. Let's have a look at this.

Genesis 1

You're probably aware that Genesis 1, the wonderful opening chapter of the Old Testament, is full of repetition. It is there to make a point, to make us sit up and listen, to grasp something that is fundamentally significant. If you read and consider the passage you'll see that the whole narrative of Genesis 1:1—2:3 is structured around diverse repetitions that drive the reader to pause and to consider. For example, the concluding words, 'Thus the heavens and the earth were completed in all their vast array. By the seventh day God had finished the work he had been doing' (Genesis 2:1–2) reflect the opening verse (the topic sentence), 'In the beginning God created the heavens and the earth' (Genesis 1:1). The creation narrative is bookended, then, by the statement that it is God whom has created everything that there is. In between the bookends, we have a literary/ theological narrative emphasising again and again that this is the case – and it does so through repetition.

The repetitions underline that God is clearly the subject, that he is in control. It is God who the writer wants us to focus on from beginning to end, so the repeated phrases generally point in that direction. Notice this in the following:

- The phrase 'God said' begins the work of each day: 1:3, 6, 9, 14, 20, 24 (see also, 1:11, 22, 26 and 28).
- 'God made': 1:7, 16, 25.
- 'God called': 1:5, 8, 10.
- 'God blessed': 1:22, 28, 2:3.
- 'God saw that it was good' (or 'very good'): 1:10, 12, 18, 21, 25, 31.

These repeated phrases demonstrate and emphasise the Lord's involvement, his creativity, his powerful creating – noticeably through the spoken word: God said, God called, God blessed. He says, 'Let there be' or 'Let them' nine times in chapter 1 (vv. 3, 6, 9, 11, 14, 15, 20, 24, 26). And the simple, short yet profound emphatic phrase 'And it was so' (vv. 7, 9, 11, 15, 30) stresses the apparent ease of creation, the certainty of it too. The poetic framework or pattern involves the repetition of the days – beginning and ending, evening and morning (vv. 5, 8, 13, 19, 23) – and the numbering of them: 'the first day' (v. 5), 'the second day' (v. 8), 'the third day' (v. 13) and so on, to the day on which the Lord rests from creating, the blessed day (2:2–3).

The beautiful and careful poetic structure of Genesis 1 is obvious. It's there to make a point: that the Lord is sovereign, that he and no other created all that there is, that he brings order out of chaos (see Genesis 1:2) and that he has set humanity into an entirely suitable, ordered, plentiful and 'good' environment in which they are to reflect the Lord, in whose image they are made (1:27), and ultimately to share in and to enjoy the divine rest.

It's no accident that John starts his gospel by repeating the iconic Genesis words, 'In the beginning' (John 1:1), for he wants to stress the fact that in the Word made flesh, Jesus Christ, a new creation is being inaugurated; that out of the chaos of sinful lives and situations the sovereign, creating God comes to make a new humanity – so he repeats from the Genesis account the themes of life and light (vv. 4, 5, 7, 8, 9) and of creation itself (v. 3). The close repetition of Genesis 1 had left its divinely commissioned mark on the tradition and, many generations later, John recalls this and utilises it to introduce Jesus, through whom comes a new order of things, a new creation in which dwells righteousness, grace and truth.

Repeated passages or stories

In reading through the Bible we'll find that whole lengthy passages or stories are repeated. For example, the books of Kings and Chronicles deal with roughly the same material, but on a careful reading we notice that they look at each incident from a different perspective. 1 and 2 Kings were written more confidently before the people of God were forced into exile, 1 and 2 Chronicles after that terrible and dislocating event. Why not dip into them, looking at the same incidents and see if you can discover the difference?

Similarly, the ten commandments are repeated in the Pentateuch (the first five books of the Bible), indicating their importance to the new community of God's people, to succeeding generations and to us. However, they come with a different perspective. In Exodus 20, the account of God giving the commandments to the people on their release from slavery in Egypt, the commandment concerning the sabbath day says that they are to keep it holy because the Lord made it so:

> In six days the Lord made the heavens and the earth, the
> sea, and all that is in them, but he rested on the seventh day.
> Therefore the Lord blessed the Sabbath day and made it holy.
> EXODUS 20:11

In the later book, Deuteronomy, the commandments are repeated –
indicating their importance to the well-being of the people – but the
sabbath commandment is said to have been given for a different
reason:

> Remember that you were slaves in Egypt and that the Lord
> your God brought you out of there with a mighty hand
> and an outstretched arm. Therefore the Lord your God has
> commanded you to observe the Sabbath day.
> DEUTERONOMY 5:15

This needn't trouble us; it's proof of a developing theology or
understanding. The sabbath day commandment comes from a
creating God who rested on the seventh day and redeemed his
people on that same day, creating a community and bringing them
into rest.

The largest parts of scripture that are repeated – sometimes word
for word – are the four gospels in the New Testament. Each one gives
the story of Jesus and declares the saving significance of his life
and death for those who believe. Some commentators suggest that
having four gospels gives credibility to the life of Jesus, their subject.
Having four, they work as witnesses to the truth of what is being
told, just as having two or three witnesses to a crime establishes the
matter in Old Testament law (see Deuteronomy 19:15). Some suggest
that having multiple gospels emphasises the importance of the
person of Jesus Christ, or that each gospel speaks to a different faith
community with differing needs and concerns. There may be truth
in each of these assertions, but in terms of reading and engaging
with the gospels it's worth noticing that having four gospels allows
for different approaches to the life and ministry of Jesus Christ – a

thought that we'll consider again later (see chapter 24, 'Perspectives on Jesus', on page 151). Whichever of these opinions is true, my advice is that we read the gospels as much as we can, again and again – they are, after all, our primary documents on our Saviour's life and teaching.

Repeated phrases

Some phrases are repeated in scripture and sometimes seem to us to be simple repetition for repetition's sake. But we've already come to see that repetition has a purpose. So when we read in Exodus the phrase 'The Lord said to Moses' at least 14 times,[72] we are reminded time and again that Moses has the Lord's authority, that he comes as God's representative – after all, the words indicate that the Lord has revealed himself to him and spoken the words directly to him before Moses tells the people. The repetition validates Moses as God's spokesman. Again, throughout the Pentateuch the statement 'I am the Lord your God, who brought you out of the land of Egypt' is repeated at crucial moments,[73] revealing and emphasising the Lord's relationship of redemptive love with the Israelites.

Two other repetitions in the Old Testament are worth mentioning. If you read 1 Kings 19:9–13, you'll see that Elijah has run away from his enemies and is depressed because he fears for his life, even though he has recently experienced the miraculous working of God against the prophets of Baal on Mount Carmel. Elijah is feeling sorry for himself: he's been zealous, rejected and isolated and is now afraid (v. 10). In this chapter the Lord graciously approaches his prophet asking, 'What are you doing here, Elijah?' (v. 9). Exactly the same question is asked a little later (v. 13). Between these enquiries God reveals himself, not in tearing wind, earthquake or blistering fire, but in 'a gentle whisper' (v. 12). The question, repeated as it is, is important. The Lord is asking why Elijah is in the state he finds him. Why does he fear? Where is his prophetic faith? How will he continue in his calling?

Again, in Psalm 130 we have a phrase repeated for poetic emphasis. The psalmist, feeling dejected, crying to the Lord for attention (v. 2), waiting for forgiveness and peace, says:

> I wait for the Lord, my whole being waits,
>   and in his word I put my hope.
> I wait for the Lord
>   more than watchmen wait for the morning,
>   more than watchmen wait for the morning.
>
> PSALM 130:5–6

In this beautiful poetic structure of repetition, the psalmist makes us wait, to feel how it feels, to empathise with his situation, to know what waiting is like: slow, determined, watchful, hopeful – but ultimately certain. The repeated phrase 'more than watchmen wait for the morning' portrays the almost intolerable waiting for an answer, but also the confidence that it will come.

In Matthew's gospel, Jesus repeats the phrase 'My Father who is in heaven', indicating his relationship with God and his genuine authority as God's Son.[74] In John's gospel, Jesus repeats the phrase 'these things I have spoken to you' to underline his teaching authority and himself as the source of truth. Notice how these are concentrated in chapter 16, just before his arrest and the coming to the disciples of the Holy Spirit to continue Christ's work.[75]

Repetition in the Bible is an important feature of its teaching style. It's there to help us think more, to pause, to engage. It will do that more effectively if we read scripture aware of its purpose.

See for yourself

- Read Genesis 5. What phrase is repeated (8 times)? Can you see why this might be so, especially with the contrast to Enoch (v. 24) and the reminder of the curse (v. 29)? Why is the author repeating this phrase? Does this add meaning and weight to this beautifully structured and shaped chapter – a chapter we might otherwise have been tempted to skip over?

- What does the repetition add to Exodus 40?
- Read through the psalms and discover poetic repetition there.
- Read a couple of the gospels and see where and how they repeat incidents in the life of Christ.

24

Perspectives on Jesus: above or below?

Have you ever noticed that John's gospel seems different from the other three (Matthew, Mark and Luke), which we call the synoptic gospels? Whereas Matthew begins with what looks like a rather mundane genealogy, Mark with the baptism of Jesus and Luke with his birth, John begins with the grand and evocatively theological sentence, 'In the beginning was the Word, and the Word was with God, and the Word was God' (John 1:1). If we can discern why there is a difference, we'll be better situated to engage more fully with each of the gospels – and, ultimately, it's a difference not of theology but of perspective.

Wolfhart Pannenberg, in his seminal writing on Jesus, *Jesus – God and Man*,[76] suggests that it's a difference of looking either 'from below' or 'from above'. Let's simplify his rather complex idea.

When we're reading the synoptic gospels we can do so from the perspective of the disciples, 'from below', from the human angle first: Jesus born, visited by shepherds and the Magi; Jesus baptised, preaching and curing others; Jesus gathering disciples and sending them out; predicting his death, suffering, dying and being raised to life and ascension. There are definitely hints about who Jesus is throughout these gospels, indicating his messiahship, for example, but there is a definite growth in the disciples' understanding as each gospel proceeds. These culminate with Christ's resurrection, after which they worship him (Matthew 28:17; Luke 24:52), but they remain 'bewildered' (Mark 16:8). Each of these gospel writers wants us to journey with the disciples, picking up hints, beginning to realise, but not knowing fully until Jesus' resurrection, that this is the Son of God. Each of these gospels leads the reader tentatively towards worshipping the resurrected Jesus.

John's gospel is very different. It starts, 'In the beginning was the Word, and the Word was with God, and the Word was God' (John 1:1). Whereas the other writers narrate 'from below', from the earthly walk of Jesus, John starts 'from above', from the heavenly existence. We are in no doubt as to who Jesus is and that this one who 'became flesh and made his dwelling among us' is God – the prologue spells this out for us, finally identifying the human Jesus with the Word who is God (see v. 17). John speaks with confidence and dogmatically: 'No-one has ever seen God, but the one and only Son, who is himself God' (v. 18) – and this is Jesus Christ. Whereas the other gospel writers present Jesus and lead us slowly to that conclusion, John tells us what we're looking at – Jesus is God. Now we need to pay attention, given what we know.

Many of the stories and the teaching that John narrates are the same as in the other gospels, but there are significant differences. For example, John speaks of only seven miracles performed by Jesus, using the term 'signs' (*semeia*) rather than 'mighty works' (*dunameis*), as the synoptics generally do. The first sign that John recounts is Jesus' changing water into the finest wine in Cana, called a sign 'through which he revealed his glory' (John 2:11).[77] This recalls for us the glory that was spoken of in the prologue: 'We have seen his glory, the glory of the one and only Son, who came from the Father, full of grace and truth' (John 1:14). Notice, too, that the disciples are said to believe in him.Unlike the synoptics, John has Jesus revealing himself as the Son of God time and again throughout his gospel. In a very real sense it culminates with Thomas' post-resurrection assertion and affirmation of faith, 'My Lord and my God!' (John 20:28).

Can you see why we might say that the synoptic gospels look at the life of Jesus 'from below' (to use Pannenberg's helpful phrase) and that John comes at it 'from above'? John declares, in an almost creedal fashion, that Jesus is God: that he comes from above, from heaven, from glory, into the world he himself has made (see John 1:3). Because of this, it is often said that John's gospel has a descent–ascent shape to it. The Word descends to dwell among us, then ascends to be with the Father again.

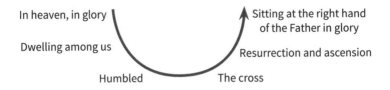

In heaven, in glory

Dwelling among us

Humbled

Sitting at the right hand of the Father in glory

Resurrection and ascension

The cross

This is implied in the prologue to the gospel. It is hinted at in the use of 'sign' for miracle. It also resurfaces at times throughout the narrative. One such time is in Jesus' prayer in John 17, in which Jesus speaks of himself as being sent by God (vv. 3, 18) and as returning to the Father (vv. 11, 13). Another clear indication comes a little earlier at the time of Jesus washing his disciples' feet, in the phrase, 'Jesus knew... that he had come from God and was returning to God' (John 13:3). Earlier still, in chapter 6, the descent–ascent motif is apparent in Jesus' own words: 'For I have come down from heaven' (v. 38); 'I am the bread that came down from heaven' (v. 41); 'What if you see the Son of Man [that is, Jesus himself] ascend to where he was before' (v. 62). Jesus came down to do the work of him who sent him, and will be raised to sit again at his right hand on the accomplishment of that work. Unlike the other gospels, John's gospel is explicit about this descent–ascent shape to Jesus' life, and it's worth noticing when we engage with John's account.

It's worth noticing, too, that John considers Jesus' cross as part and parcel of his glorification and not so much as part of the humiliation, as we might expect – after all, this aspect of Jesus' teaching baffled the disciples too! In predicting his death, Jesus comments that 'the hour has come for the Son of Man to be glorified' (John 12:23). When Judas left the company of disciples to betray Jesus, the Lord says, 'Now is the Son of Man glorified and God is glorified in him' (13:31; see also 17:1–5). In some ways we would prefer the death of Jesus to be part of his humiliation, his descent, but John emphasises that it is actually part of his exaltation, his glorification, his ascent.

Interestingly, the apostle Paul shapes the life of Jesus similarly in his letter to the Philippian church. Here, he probably uses a contemporary Christian hymn. We can see that his thought is not identical to John's, but he employs a similar descent–ascent (or in this case, humbled–exalted) shape:

Who, being in very nature God,
    did not consider equality with God
    something to be used to his own advantage;
rather, he made himself nothing
    by taking the very nature of a servant,
    being made in human likeness.
And being found in appearance as a human being,
    he humbled himself
    by becoming obedient to death –
    even death on a cross!

Therefore God exalted him to the highest place
    and gave him the name that is above every name,
that at the name of Jesus every knee should bow,
    in heaven and on earth and under the earth,
and every tongue acknowledge that Jesus Christ is Lord,
    to the glory of God the Father.
PHILIPPIANS 2:6–11

See for yourself

Read through the gospels slowly, each in turn, and see the difference in perspective: the synoptic gospels view Jesus 'from below'; John's gospel views him 'from above'. How does this difference engage you as the reader? How does each approach underline who Jesus is and lead to our faith-response to his life?

25

The boring bits: a love of lists and detail

In his excellent anecdotal book *Could This Be God?*, Brian Harris asks readers what they find to be the most boring bits in the Bible, and he suggests that the catalogues of names might be top of the list. Interestingly, he goes on to say that Jews find genealogies among the most interesting parts of scripture, as they speak about who a person is: 'It has to do with knowing your roots, your place in history and your continuity with the past… It's also a reminder that, contrary to the individualism of our day, none of us really lives in isolation.'[78]

You can see that when you read, for example, Matthew's opening chapter, outlining the genealogy of Jesus: 'This is the genealogy of Jesus the Messiah the son of David, the son of Abraham' (Matthew 1:1) – 17 verses (as long as John's prologue) on the ancestors of Jesus Christ. Reading these verses, it's clear what Matthew wants us to see: the significance of the person whose life he is going to relate. The mention of King David and of the patriarch Abraham in Jesus' line is significant. Here is the whole weight of Old Testament thinking and hoping, tradition and prophecy, and, with God's own plan in Israel's history lying behind the birth of Jesus, the chapter continues, 'This is how the birth of Jesus the Messiah came about' (Matthew 1:18).

But there are other lists which may be more difficult to get excited about. Take, for example, the lists of those who travelled with Jacob to Egypt (Genesis 46), or the names listed at the first census after leaving Egypt (Numbers 1) or at the second (Numbers 26), or the men sent to explore Canaan (Numbers 13), or the divisions of priests, musicians, gatekeepers and so on (1 Chronicles 24—26). The scripture writers loved lists of names, names that mean next to nothing to us today. How do we read them? Allow me to outline my approach and see if it helps your engagement with these and other similar portions of scripture.

Like you, probably, I found these lists of names daunting, tedious and even unreadable until I thought about it a bit more. Let me explain with an illustration. The Menin Gate in Ypres, Belgium, is a war memorial for those soldiers who died in World War I and are left with no known grave. At the end of each day, the town of Ypres remembers these by a simple and short service of remembrance, together with the last post being played. It commemorates well over 50,000 troops, killed in action. Their names are engraved upon the triumphal arch in alphabetical order. It's interesting that when you stand beneath that arch, confronted with the terrible number of names, your instinct is actually to read them and to muse on who they were, that they were 'real' like you, that they were missed and mourned. They 'come alive' to your imagination, each one seeming somehow significant.

I find the same thing when confronted with lists of names in scripture. I read them slowly (against my natural instinct to 'get this done'). Each person was significant. Each name represents a person loved by family and friends, loved and called by God, who saved them out of captivity in Egypt and gave them freedom.

I was reminded of this in reading 3 John, in which the writer concludes, 'Peace to you. The friends here send their greetings. Greet the friends there by name' (3 John 14) – greet them *by name*! Names are incredibly important. Names represent human beings, caught up in the things of their lives, divinely called within a nation, a people. Notice how this helps in the following example. Try reading it slowly and thoughtfully.

The divisions of the gatekeepers:

> from the Korahites: Meshelemiah son of Kore, one of the sons of Asaph.

Meshelemiah had sons:

> Zechariah the firstborn,
> Jediael the second,
> Zebadiah the third,
> Jathniel the fourth,
> Elam the fifth,
> Jehohanan the sixth
> and Eliehoenai the seventh.

1 CHRONICLES 26:1–3

Imagine that these names signify men who were proud to be called gatekeepers of the temple of the Lord. This was their vocation before the Lord. Later, we are informed that Zechariah (the firstborn in the list) was 'a wise counsellor' who, by lot, was given the north gate to guard (v. 14), a detail that embellishes our view of him.

Just as the lists of names can become an obstacle to reading, so too can seemingly endless details. Scripture writers love them! Do you recall the details for manufacturing the ark in which Noah and his family found redemption (Genesis 6:14–16)? These pale into insignificance compared to the details for constructing the tabernacle and its utensils and accoutrements that go on for several chapters (Exodus 36–40) and Ezekiel's reimagining of the temple much later in Israel's history (Ezekiel 40). A verse in the last of these references is perhaps instructive for us in seeking to engage with these texts. The Lord says to the prophet Ezekiel the following:

> Son of man, describe the temple to the people of Israel, that they may be ashamed of their sins. Let them consider its perfection, and if they are ashamed of all they have done, make known to them the design of the temple.

EZEKIEL 43:10–11

If nothing else, this reminds us that there is a particular purpose about the details that biblical writers include. For instance, the prophet here is told to describe the temple *in order* that the Israelites would be ashamed. And specifically, they are to 'consider its perfection'. The details, which we wish to merely step over in our reading, these very details indicate perfection! There is something holy about this (see v. 12); the Lord is involved; it is his dwelling among his people.

And so too with the tabernacle earlier. When the tabernacle had been built to divine specifications, when Moses had 'finished the work' (Exodus 40:33), *then* the Lord 'covered the tent of meeting and the glory of the Lord filled the tabernacle' (v. 34), but not before. This is reflected in John's revelation of the new heaven and the new earth, in which he describes in detail the new Jerusalem, the bride of Christ – perfectly formed, finished, complete – in which the glory of the Lord will be present and his people will see his face (see Revelation 21:9—22:5).

Lists of names, numbers and details will always be somewhat problematic for those who wish to engage with scripture. They probably won't ever be the passages that take us confidently and joyfully out into the world to be disciples of Jesus today. But they do express something of the original faith of the writers, and we should certainly respect that, if we can. Look for their purpose. Consider who these people were who to us filter down as names on a page. Read slowly and thoughtfully; try not to rush or bypass these 'boring bits'.

26

Lastly: the final things before the end

When we read scripture we soon learn that those who wrote it had an eye on the end, the final things, what theologians call 'eschatology'. The word 'eschatology' comes from the Greek word meaning the last in a list or sequence of things or events; and not simply the last, but those things or events that determine the rest (in the same way, for example, as a wedding will determine the planning and events leading up to it). In this context it refers to those events that will usher in the consummation of God's redemptive plan, and it entails things like death, the Lord's return, judgement, resurrection, angels, trumpet calls, the defeat of evil and so on (see 1 Thessalonians 4:13–18, for instance). Both Old Testament and New Testament believers looked forward to it; they longed for its occurrence – the appearing of God and his final victory (see Zephaniah 3:20; Revelation 22:20). Passages that relate to this topic are full of hope and certainty, of warning and expectant joy. But they are also full of complexity.

This certainly isn't the place to begin to unravel biblical eschatology, even if we could. I would suggest, however, that you don't get too caught up in its complex imagery and suggestive ideas at this stage. Try to keep things as simple as possible; get the gist, the general idea of what's being said. However, we should look at two matters that will help us read the Bible in a more engaged way: that the situation is more complex than imagined and that the last things have already started with Jesus.

The situation is more complex than imagined

Have you noticed that the Old Testament prophets speak of the last day quite often, speaking of it as 'that day' or 'the day of the Lord' and so on? The prophet Zephaniah, for example, declares that 'the great day of the Lord is near – near and coming quickly' (Zephaniah 1:14). Obadiah says the same: 'The day of the Lord is near for all nations' (v. 15), continuing, 'The kingdom will be the Lord's' (v. 21). Jeremiah is more expansive, with a prophetic suggestion of the coming of Jesus himself:

'The days are coming,' declares the Lord,
   'when I will raise up for David a righteous Branch,
a King who will reign wisely
   and do what is just and right in the land.
In his days Judah will be saved
   and Israel will live in safety.
This is the name by which he will be called:
   The Lord Our Righteous Saviour.'

JEREMIAH 23:5–6

Without going into too much detail,[79] it appears that the Old Testament writers believed that on 'that day' things would be different, that wrongs would be abruptly righted, that Israel would be safe. And this belief became tied up with the notion that the Messiah ('the son of man' of Daniel 7:13–14) was to come; that at his appearance the old age would cease and a new age would dawn. This, they thought, would be a linear happening.

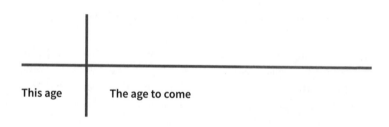

This age | The age to come

However, with the coming of Jesus the Messiah (notice how explicit this is in Matthew 1:1, 18) things were not that simple. Indeed, they were far more complex than the Old Testament writers could have imagined. For with him came the kingdom of God and the new age was inaugurated, but for now the old age unexpectedly continued. Therefore, the New Testament writers complicate the picture because they discern that with the coming of Messiah Jesus the old scheme is too simple to explain the actual event.

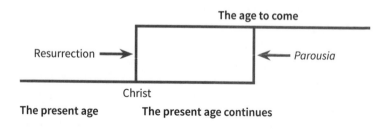

This diagram indicates the continuance of the present age, but shows too that the new age has actually begun with Christ – and specifically with his resurrection and ascension and the presence of the Holy Spirit. Both ages will continue side by side until the second coming of Jesus (the *parousia*), at which point the old will be finished forever. Paul indicates this new scheme, the coexistence between the ages, in his letter to the Galatian church, in which he speaks of Jesus, saying that he 'gave himself for our sins to rescue us from the present evil age, according to the will of our God and Father, to whom be glory forever and ever. Amen' (Galatians 1:4–5). He speaks of both ages in Ephesians 1:21 and implies it in 1 Corinthians 2:6–7 and 2 Corinthians 4:4.

Why not pause for a moment and read the following Old Testament passages with this in mind?

- Jeremiah 23:1–8
- Joel 2:28–32
- Obadiah
- Zephaniah 1:7–18

Before we make anything of this, let's look at the second thing that we should be aware of in the tricky area of eschatology.

The last things have already started with Jesus

Again and again throughout this book we've noted the central importance of Jesus. It's worth keeping this important point in view here too. With Jesus' coming the new age dawns. Believers, says the apostle Paul, are somehow spiritually located 'in Christ'. If you read Ephesians 1:3–14, for example, you'll see what I mean. Much of this passage is a single sentence in the original, and in it no fewer than eleven times the apostle draws attention to our attachment to and the significance of Jesus Christ:

- We are blessed with spiritual blessings in Christ (v. 3).
- We are chosen in Christ (v. 4).
- God predestined us through Jesus Christ (v. 5).
- God has given us grace through Jesus, 'the One he loves' (v. 6).
- We have redemption through Christ's death (v. 7).
- God's purposes come through Christ (v. 9).
- The unity of all things in heaven and earth comes through Christ (v. 10).
- We were chosen in Christ (v. 11).

- We put our hope in Christ (v. 12).
- We're included 'in Christ' (v. 13).
- We were marked in him with a seal, the Holy Spirit (v. 13).

Amazing! And the apostle underlines the fact that because of this we live already 'in the heavenly realms' (v. 3). With Jesus the future age has dawned, and it already affects us, his disciples. We are located in the heavenly realms because we are located in Christ by grace. So eschatology – the last things – has already had its effect on us as believers. Paul spells this out for us:

> But because of his great love for us, God, who is rich in mercy, made us alive with Christ even when we were dead in transgressions – it is by grace you have been saved. And God raised us up with Christ and seated us with him in the heavenly realms in Christ Jesus.
> EPHESIANS 2:4–6

Elsewhere Paul speaks of our citizenship being in heaven (Philippians 3:20) and exhorts believers to set their hearts on things above *because* they 'have been raised with Christ' (Colossians 3:1).

This is what New Testament scholars call 'the already/not yet' aspect of Christian existence. We are already in the heavenlies with Christ, but not yet fully so. Paul uses several images to convey this. One of the images he employs is of the first fruits of the harvest. Imagine a farmer standing in front of his field of wheat. The whole field is ready to harvest, but with a single swing of the sickle he cuts down and takes the first fruit of the crop. This relatively small amount represents the fullness of the field's abundance; it indicates that the rest is certain – now and not yet. Paul also employs the image of a deposit that guarantees our inheritance, the first payment of all the rest – now and not yet. The Holy Spirit is that first fruit (Romans 8:23); he is that deposit (2 Corinthians 5:5; Ephesians 1:14). In Jesus Christ we have everything, and the Holy Spirit is the seal of guarantee.

Although this is a complex subject, it gives us a handle with which to engage scripture, for we live in the tension between the now and the not yet. We live now in the kingdom; we have the Holy Spirit; we are made righteous; we dwell in the heavenly realm with Christ. But as we read scripture, at times we can feel like failures because we simply don't live up to all that these aspects of our salvation in Christ suggest.

The tension is palpable for Paul, for example: 'For what I want to do I do not do, but what I hate I do… For I do not do the good I want to do, but the evil I do not want to do – this I keep on doing' (Romans 7:15, 19). His lament comes to a sudden stop as he contemplates what it means to be in Christ: 'Who will rescue me from this body of death? Thanks be to God, who delivers me through Jesus Christ our Lord!' (vv. 24–25). Later, seeking to encourage godliness in others, Paul urges them to set their 'minds on things above' not on earthly things: 'For you died,' he says, 'and your life is now hidden with Christ in God' (Colossians 3:2–3).

So don't be put off reading scripture because of its demands. It is true that the Lord is holy and he calls us to be holy, too. But try to engage with the Bible's call to godly living, to be like Jesus Christ, within the eschatological reality of our present Christian experience – though we are 'in Christ' and have the Holy Spirit, we still have a long way to go. Allow the Bible's message to encourage you to persist in godliness, not to give up. What we have now is a promise of what is not yet. Persevere in your discipleship. The apostle Paul writes,

> Not that I have already obtained all this, or have already arrived at my goal, but I press on to take hold of that for which Christ Jesus took hold of me… Forgetting what is behind and straining towards what is ahead, I press on towards the goal to win the prize for which God has called me heavenwards in Christ Jesus.
>
> PHILIPPIANS 3:12–14

See for yourself

Why not read the following passages with these aspects of eschatology, the last things, in mind? How does the thought of being in the heavenlies already in Christ affect your reading? How is the Holy Spirit's activity involved in what's being said? Does the eschatological thinking of scripture give at least a foothold into engaging with these passages and applying them to your own life?

- Romans 7:7–25
- Ephesians 1:1–14
- Philippians 3:17–21
- 2 Peter 3

Conclusion: reading scripture – to what end?

Why do we read the Bible? Why do we want to be biblically literate? Why make the effort to engage with the text? By way of conclusion, let me suggest some answers to this. You'll see that this list is not at all exhaustive, just suggestive of some emphases that you've already discovered in this book.

Reading the Bible and our worship

As far as I can tell, the church has always considered the reading of scripture as a part of Christian worship. That is, when we read the Bible with a faithful and trusting spirit, when we engage with God's word, seeking to know more of him and his wonderful ways, we worship the Lord. And the Lord is pleased with our worship. Even the rather mechanical strategies outlined above should all conclude with doxology, the praise of God the Father, as we learn more about him and the redemption that he has wrought through Jesus Christ.

May our reading, then, be doxological, rebounding to his glory:

Oh, how I love your law!
I meditate on it all day long...

Accept, Lord, the willing praise of my mouth.
PSALM 119:97, 108

Worship – that is the primary reason for reading scripture and engaging with it: the worship of the God of scripture, the one who graciously reveals himself to us through scripture, the one who deserves all our worship and praise.

Reading the Bible and our sanctification

We read scripture, too, in order to be conformed to the image of God's Son, Jesus Christ. We seek to know something of his grace, his trust, his humility, his compassion, his goodness, his wisdom and his generous, inclusive spirit. Echoing the Leviticus code, 'Be holy because I, the Lord your God, am holy' (see Leviticus 19:2, for instance), Jesus demands that we be like God, the Father: 'Be perfect, therefore, as your heavenly Father is perfect' (Matthew 5:48). We seek this perfection through knowing Jesus and by being disciples of him, by seeing him in scripture and in taking upon ourselves his example, as much as we are able. Jesus prays, 'Sanctify them by the truth; your word is truth' (John 17:17).

May our reading lead to godliness and a genuine imitation of Christ.

Reading the Bible and our encouragement in hardships

We read scripture to strengthen ourselves, or rather for the Lord to strengthen us, in difficult times. We learn what it is to rest in the word of God, the promises of God, when all around us is falling apart, when health is failing, when redundancy hits, when old age takes its toll, when death and grief encroach into our lives and hurt us. We remember the example of Jesus (1 Peter 3:17–18), we lean upon the comfort that the Lord gives (2 Corinthians 1:3–5), we recall – perhaps, against what we presently observe – that God is faithful and loving (Lamentations 3:21–26) and we wait upon him with hope and trust. The psalmist asks where could he go for help and his answer is pertinent for us.

I lift up my eyes to the mountains –
     where does my help come from?
My help comes from the Lord,
     the Maker of heaven and earth.
PSALM 121:1–2

It isn't the reading of the Bible, per se, that helps us, but the fact that the Bible reveals to us God behind the word ('the Maker of heaven and earth') who sustains us, for through reading the Bible we lean into God himself, and he becomes very present to us in every circumstance.

May the reading of scripture encourage us in him during difficult times.

Reading the Bible and trust of sins forgiven

We read scripture to help us to deal with our own sin and consciences. Scripture points out sin in a bold way. A vulnerable reading of it reveals our sin to us: 'I gain understanding from your precepts,' says the psalmist, '*therefore* I hate every wrong path' (Psalm 119:104, my emphasis). But the same scripture encourages us to trust that those sins are dealt with in Christ, that we are a new creation, temples of the Holy Spirit – they encourage us to be holy (see Psalm 51; Colossians 3), knowing that our sins are forgiven by a gracious God.

He does not treat us as our sins deserve
     or repay us according to our iniquities.
For as high as the heavens are above the earth,
     so great is his love for those who fear him;

as far as the east is from the west,
so far has he removed our transgressions from us.

PSALM 103:10–12

May our reading be faithfully vulnerable to the point of recognising our sins and the love of God that covers them in Christ.

Reading the Bible and testifying to God's love

We read scripture to help us to speak about our experience of God to those who have not yet come to faith in Jesus Christ. The apostle Peter says that disciples should 'always be prepared to give an answer to everyone who asks you to give the reason for the hope that you have' (1 Peter 3:15). Previously, in his last discourses, Jesus himself promises his disciples that the Spirit of truth will come and guide them into all truth (John 16:13). This is not to say that we should use the Bible as a textbook or a rule book, gleaning from it propositions and arguments to use 'against' those who don't yet believe – not at all! The truth that the Spirit guides us into is the truth of God: it is relational; it breathes love and grace; it enables us to speak of Jesus Christ and our relationship with him and of his goodness towards us and to the world.

May our reading be filled with a faithful acquisition of truth and encourage in us an openness to speak about what we know and have experienced of the love of God in Jesus Christ.

Bible reading and social justice

The scriptures speak often of the need for God's people to be involved in justice and compassion. The Old Testament teaching is summed up in Micah's well-known words:

He has shown all you people what is good.

> And what does the Lord require of you?
> To act justly and to love mercy
>   and to walk humbly with your God.
>
> MICAH 6:8

Amos pleads for justice to 'roll on like a river, righteousness like a never-failing stream!' (Amos 5:24). Jesus even identifies himself with those in desperate need: the homeless, the thirsty, the stranger, the naked and the sick (Matthew 25:45).

May our reading of scripture fill us with genuine, Spirit-given compassion for those in need so that we might live as Jesus demands.

* * *

I hope that this book on how to read the Bible has been helpful. If you've found it so, why not suggest to your home group, your leadership group or your preaching team that they spend some time engaging with the ideas in it? We need a biblically literate church today. May God grant us such to his glory and the growth of his kingdom.

Notes

1 For books on such matters, I suggest Krish Kandiah, *Paradoxology. Why Christianity was never meant to be simple* (Hodder, 2015); Gordon Fee and Douglas Stuart, *How to Read the Bible for All its Worth* (Zondervan, 2003); Gordon Fee and Douglas Stuart, *How to Read the Bible Book by Book* (Zondervan, 2002); Helen Paynter, *God of Violence Yesterday, God of Love Today?* (BRF, 2019).

2 Philip Yancey, *The Bible Jesus Read* (Zondervan, 1999), p. 18.

3 Larry D. Hart, *Truth Aflame: A balanced theology for Evangelicals and Charismatics* (Thomas Nelson, 1999), p. 35.

4 Clive Field, 'Is the Bible becoming a closed book? British opinion poll evidence', *Journal of Contemporary Religion* 29.3 (2014), pp. 503–528. I recommend Imogen Ball's paper for The London Institute for Contemporary Christianity, 'Biblical literacy or biblical literacies? Searching for biblical literacy in unexpected places' for a well-reasoned and nuanced view of the situation. For *Pass It On*, see **biblesociety.org.uk/what-we-do/england-and-wales/pass-it-on-report**.

5 Peter M. Phillips, *Engaging the Word: Biblical literacy and Christian discipleship* (BRF, 2017), chapter 2.

6 Karl Barth, *Witness to the Word: A commentary on John 1* (Wipf and Stock, 2003), p. 6. On the historicity and specificity of the writer, see also Karl Rahner, *Foundations of the Christian Faith* (Darton, Longmann and Todd, 1978), pp. 376–77.

7 Barth, *Witness to the Word*, p. 6.

8 See Barth, *Church Dogmatics* (T&T Clark, 1975), 1.1, p. 117.

9 See Gordon Spykman, *Reformational Theology* (Eerdmans, 1992), pp. 76–88.

10 Eugene Peterson, *Eat This Book: The art of spiritual reading* (Hodder and Stoughton, 2006), p. 24.

11 Geoffrey Wainwright, *Doxology: A systematic theology – the praise of God in worship, doctrine and life* (Epworth Press, 1980), p. 149.

12   Wainwright, *Doxology*, p. 150.

13   Wainwright, *Doxology*, pp. 167–168 (see also p. 178).

14   Phillips, *Engaging the Word*, p. 101. See chapter 1 for a brief examination of the other models.

15   Phillips, *Engaging the Word*, p. 24 (see also, p. 107).

16   Millard Erickson, *Christian Theology* (Baker Academic, 2013), pp. 199–200; my emphasis.

17   Wolfhart Pannenberg, *Systematic Theology*, volume 1 (translated by Geoffrey Bromiley; Eerdmans, 1991), pp. 189, 225; original emphasis (see also p. 233).

18   See Barth, *Church Dogmatics* 1.1, pp. 193–94.

19   John Vincent Taylor, *The Christlike God* (SCM, 2011).

20   Barth, *Witness to the Word*, p. 26; Andrew D. Mayes, *Sensing the Divine: John's word made flesh* (BRF, 2019), p. 50, respectively.

21   Hart, *Truth Aflame*, p. 34.

22   We know, for instance, that one of the apostle Paul's letters is missing. See also, for example, 1 Kings 15:31 and 2 Chronicles 35:25. Also, and particularly, John 20:30: Jesus performed revelatory miracles ('signs') that we know nothing of, but which revealed who he is to those present.

23   Emil Brunner, *Truth as Encounter* (SCM, 1964), p. 109.

24   Barth, *Witness to the Word*, p. 16.

25   Hart, *Truth Aflame*, p. 34.

26   Clark H. Pinnock and Robert C. Brow, *Unbounded Love: A good news theology for the 21st century* (InterVarsity Press, 1994), pp. 32–33; emphasis original. Later, they say that 'scripture gives access to revelation' (p. 160).

27   Stephen E. Fowl, *Theological Interpretation of Scripture* (Cascade Books, 2009), pp. 11–12.

28   Fowl, *Theological Interpretation of Scripture*, p. 12.

29   Stanley J. Grenz, *Theology for the Community of God* (Eerdmans, 2000), p. 154.

30   Rahner, *Foundations of the Christian Faith*, p. 347.

31   See also Romans 6:1–11; 2 Corinthians 3:4—4:6.

32   Eugene Peterson, *Working the Angles: The shape of pastoral integrity* (Eerdmans, 1987), p. 61.

33   Peterson, *Working the Angles*, p. 62.

34   Peterson, *Working the Angles*, p. 71.

35   Peterson, *Eat This Book*, pp. 18, 20.

36   See Phillips, *Engaging the Word*, pp. 24, 36, 107.

37 Delwin Brown, *Boundaries of Our Habitations: Tradition and theological construction* (State University of New York, 1994), pp. 78–79.

38 Peterson, *Eat This Book*, p. 27; original emphasis. In Barth's words, 'The Word convinces, converts, forces, and decides. The Word is subject not object in this action': *Witness to the Word*, p. 75.

39 Michael Green, *2 Peter and Jude* (Eerdmans, 1996), p. 91.

40 For example, Genesis 1—2; Psalm 51:10; Isaiah 51:16; John 1; Galatians 6:15; Revelation 21:5.

41 For example, Exodus 12:31—14:31; Psalm 77:13–20; Isaiah 51:10.

42 For example, Exodus 12:1–30; Isaiah 31:5; John 1:29; Luke 22:7–22.

43 Brown, *Boundaries of Our Habitation*, p. 148.

44 See, for example, Christopher J.H. Wright, *God's People in God's Land* (Eerdmans, 1990); *Walking in the Ways of the Lord* (InterVarsity Press, 1995); *Living as the People of God* (InterVarsity Press, 1984); and *The Mission of God* (InterVarsity Press, 2009), pp. 394–396. I've also based the triangular model (in the next chapter) on Wright's work. My use and application of these models, however, tangentially develops his original use and purpose.

45 Terry Hinks, *Praying the Way* (BRF, 2018), p. 170.

46 For a fuller and more satisfying summary, see Graeme Goldsworthy, *Jesus through the Old Testament: Transform your Bible understanding* (BRF, 2017), pp. 25–34.

47 Walter Brueggemann, *Genesis* (John Knox Press, 1982), pp. 82–83.

48 Brueggemann, *Genesis*, p. 83.

49 Wainwright, *Doxology*, p. 149.

50 Wolfhart Pannenberg, *Systematic Theology*, volume 2 (translated by Geoffrey Bromiley; Eerdmans, 1994), p. 57.

51 See also, for example, Philippians 3:20–21; Galatians 4:26; 2 Peter 1:1.

52 Peter Phillips has a very helpful section on this topic; see *Engaging the Word*, pp. 28–35.

53 William Shakespeare, *Romeo and Juliet*, the Prologue; from S. Wells and G. Taylor (eds), *The Oxford Shakespeare: The complete works* (Clarendon Press, 2005), p. 371; my emphasis.

54 Phillips, *Engaging the Word*, p. 30.

55 For the whole story, see Joshua 2 and 6:17.

56 On this important point, see Russ Parker, *Free to Fail* (Triangle Books, 1992), particularly, pp. 71–101.

57 See George E. Ganss SJ, *The Spiritual Exercises of Saint Ignatius: A translation and commentary* (Loyola Press, 1992); Timothy M.

Gallagher OMV, *Meditation and Contemplation. An Ignatian guide to prayer with scripture* (Crossroad, 2008); David L. Fleming SJ, *What is Ignatian Spirituality?* (Loyola Press, 2008).

58 Ganss, *The Spiritual Exercises of Saint Ignatius*, p. 21.

59 For an extended resource on this method of praying the Bible, see Michael Parsons, *Praying the Bible with Luther: A simple approach to everyday prayer* (BRF, 2017).

60 For further examples of Luther's method at work, see Parsons, *Praying the Bible with Luther*.

61 For a more detailed account of this significant subject, see Michael Parsons, 'Being precedes act: indicative and imperative in Paul's writing' in Brian S. Rosner (ed.), *Understanding Paul's Ethics: Twentieth-century approaches* (Eerdmans, 1995), pp. 217–47.

62 For example, Romans 4:16; 5:2, 20–21; 6:1, 14–15, 17; 11:5–6.

63 See, for example, Romans 9:15–16, 18, 23; 10:12–13, 20–21; 11:22, 31–32.

64 Parsons, *Praying the Bible with Luther*, pp. 97–100.

65 Of course, this conclusion makes the events of Genesis 3 even more tragic.

66 Of the 66 uses of the word 'love' in the gospels, John has 39 (Matthew has 11, Mark, 4 and Luke, 12). John 13:1 seems to sum up his intentions.

67 Christopher Wright, *The Message of Ezekiel: A new heart and a new way* (InterVarsity Press, 2001), p. 46.

68 Simon Stocks, *Psalms (Really Useful Guides)* (BRF, 2018), pp. 53–54.

69 Peterson, *Eat This Book*, pp. 27–28.

70 See David Potter's wonderful book on Job, *Is Your God Too Small? Enlarging our vision in the face of life's struggles* (BRF, 2018).

71 Some of the examples employed in this section come from **thoughtco.com/the-importance-of-repetition-in-the-bible-363290** and 'Repetition in the Bible', **lutherquest.org/redeemerpress/wp** – both accessed 6 August 2018.

72 See Exodus 6:10, 13, 29; 13:1; 14:1; 16:11; 25:1; 30:11, 17, 22; 31:1; 32:7; 33:1; 40:1.

73 See Exodus 20:2; 29:46; Leviticus 19:3; 25:38; 26:13; Numbers 15:41; Deuteronomy 5:6.

74 See, for example, Matthew 7:21; 10:32–33; 12:50; 16:17; 18:10–19.

75 See John 14:25; 15:11; 16:1, 4, 6, 25, 33.

76 Wolfhart Pannenberg, *Jesus – God and Man* (SCM, 2010). See also *Systematic Theology*, volume 2, pp. 278–97.

77   Other signs: healing the official's son (John 4:43–54), healing the invalid (5:1–15), feeding the 5,000 (6:1–15), walking on the water (6:16–24), healing the man born blind (9:1–12), raising Lazarus from the dead (11:1–44).

78   Brian Harris, *Could This Be God? Bumping into God in the everyday* (BRF, 2016), pp. 111–12.

79   On this important topic, see Michael Parsons, 'Time and location: aspects of realized eschatology, Paul, and our worship' in David J. Cohen and Michael Parsons (eds), *In Praise of Worship: An exploration of text and practice* (Pickwick, 2010), pp. 120–39.